Partnerships in Social Care

by the same author

Negotiation for Health and Social Service Professionals
Keith Fletcher
ISBN 1 85302 549 6

of related interest

Collaboration in Social Work Practice
Edited by Jenny Weinstein, Colin Whittington
and Tony Leiba
ISBN 1 84310 092 4

Collaboration in Health and Welfare
Working with Difference
Ann Loxley
ISBN 1 85302 394 9

Integrating Care for Older People
New Care for Old – A Systems Approach
Christopher Foote and Christine Stanners
Foreword by Bob Kane and Rosalie Kane
ISBN 1 84310 010 X

Developing Good Practice in Children's Services
Edited by Vicky White and John Harris
ISBN 1 84310 150 5

Competence in Social Work Practice
A Practical Guide for Professionals
Edited by Kieran O'Hagan
ISBN 1 85302 332 9

Social Work Management and Practice
Systems Principles
Second Edition
Andy Bilson and Sue Ross
ISBN 1 85302 388 4

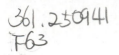

Partnerships in Social Care
A Handbook for Developing Effective Services

Keith Fletcher

Jessica Kingsley Publishers
London and Philadelphia

First published in 2006
by Jessica Kingsley Publishers
116 Pentonville Road
London N1 9JB, UK
and
400 Market Street, Suite 400
Philadelphia, PA 19106, USA

www.jkp.com

Library of Congress Cataloging in Publication Data
Fletcher, Keith (J. Keith)
    Partnerships in social care : a handbook for developing effective services / Keith Fletcher. —
1st American pbk. ed.
        p. cm.
    Includes bibliographical references and index.
    ISBN-13: 978-1-84310-380-6 (pbk. : alk. paper)
    ISBN-10: 1-84310-380-X (pbk. : alk. paper) 1. Human services—Great Britain. 2. Social
service—Great Britain. 3. Public-private sector cooperation—Great Britain. I. Title.
    HV245.F57 2006
    361.2'50941—dc22   #63703197   2006011842

British Library Cataloguing in Publication Data
A CIP catalogue record for this book is available from the British Library

ISBN-13: 978 1 84310 380 6
ISBN-10: 1 84310 380 X

Printed and bound in Great Britain by
Athenaeum Press, Gateshead, Tyne and Wear

Contents

List of Figures and Tables

Preface

Nobody writes a book like this alone and I am indebted to many friends and colleagues for their insights and ideas. If you see something here that sounds like your idea, it probably is, and I am very grateful! I would like to thank specifically a few people without whom this book would not have been written at all in its present form.

I am very grateful to Steve Jones, my editor at Jessica Kingsley Publishers, for making the process side of the book as pain-free as possible. Many people looked at all or parts of the manuscript as it emerged. Without excluding those who are not mentioned I am particularly grateful to Mike Williams, long-time friend and colleague from Partnership at Work, and Bob Woodward, even longer-time friend and ex-colleague from Social Services Inspectorate Wales, for their critiques of large parts of it. Felicity, my wife, provided support and many insights and read the manuscript critically. She also kept me focused at times when I would have preferred to stare at the wall!

A special note of thanks to my old friend Herbert Collingham. He undertook the onerous task of reading the whole draft (in more than one manifestation in parts) with the sceptical mind of a literate and logical layman. His trenchant observations concerning opacity, inconsistency and just plain rubbish have certainly enabled me to express ideas more clearly. This is the third time he has performed this service and I am extremely grateful.

For all their help, this is my book for which I accept full responsibility, warts and all. If you do find any warts let me know through our website at www.sssp.co.uk or direct by email to keith@sssp.co.uk.

I hope you enjoy the book and learn as much from reading it as I have from writing it.

PART ONE

An Overview

Introduction

SUMMARY

This book is a planning guide for politicians, managers, commissioners, service providers and professionals engaged in or setting up strategic partnerships to improve local services of social and health care and education. It deals with the necessity for partnership and its purposes. It considers the practical questions of where it should be focused, who should be involved and how it should be implemented. A book of this kind cannot possibly cover every critical issue but I have tried to provide a framework of questions to work through and some common problems people have faced and needed to resolve.

What this book is about

Partnerships in Social Care is essentially about the effective co-ordination of public sector and voluntary effort which is intended to benefit people who are in need through ill health or social vulnerability. There is little doubt that co-ordinated and jointly planned services do deliver a better, more effective service to users of health and social services, education, housing, financial support, policing and the administration of justice. But it is clear from much painful experience that this is difficult to achieve. So much effort is required to get a partnership off the ground that it sometimes absorbs the energy and effort which should be devoted to providing improved service delivery in other ways.

This book is about planning and running successful partnerships. It starts from the assumption that they should never be an end in themselves but a means of doing some things better. It follows that the nature of the partnership in a particular case should be limited to what is likely to achieve that. Above all partnership is not an ideology; it is a method.

I will explore five themes:

- Is this partnership necessary?
- What is its purpose?
- Who is involved?
- Where will it function?
- How will it work?

This book is written as a handbook rather than a series of analytical essays and is based on my experience as a consultant working with many different kinds of partnership and on research evidence about some of the things that work and some that don't. It is designed so that you can dip into it to explore the issues that are exercising you at the time. It is also constructed thematically so that you can see, almost at a glance, how each theme relates to the others.

A couple of points about the style of the book. There is a bibliography containing most of my source material other than personal experience but I have avoided numbered references and footnotes as being distracting in a book of this kind. Second, I have defined words where I have thought it helpful when they occur for the first time, and sought to remain consistent to the definitions throughout.

Third, I have dealt with the gender pronoun issue by using 'he' or 'she', 'him' or 'her' more or less alternately throughout the book. I am uncomfortable with 'they' where it is clearly singular in the context; and the 'he/she' variations are, to my mind, clumsy. So wherever you see 'she' or 'he' in this book, please remember that it has no gender significance whatsoever.

Who the book is for

The primary audience for this book will be the professionals, managers, commissioners, service providers and politicians responsible for delivering social care services. I have adopted a fairly broad definition of 'social care' to include health, adult social care, children's services, housing, police, criminal justice, education and social security. The way all these services are provided has an impact not only on the service recipient directly but on the impact of the other services as well. Partnership among key public sector and voluntary agencies working in these fields is not an option; it is a necessity. If you need some ideas about how to plan it or do it, I trust you will find them here.

You can, of course, read the book from cover to cover. It is not a tome, as you can see from looking at it in your hand, so it won't take you too long to do. On the other hand, if you prefer to get the general shape and the big ideas in brief, the synopsis, the next part of this chapter, will serve as a map for the book as a whole.

I do hope you find it helpful, stimulating, and even a little entertaining.

SYNOPSIS

The book is written in three parts.

Part One

Part One, essentially this introduction and the next chapter, gives you an overview of the key issues to consider in developing and managing a partnership. It explores in outline the five themes already mentioned. If you want an outline summary of all the ground you need to cover in developing your partnership, this is the place to start.

Part Two

Part Two explores the strategic issues. I once heard a local authority chief executive call these issues 'the motherhood and apple pie stuff which just delays the real business'. Nothing could be farther from the truth. The agenda you set yourself and negotiate with your potential partners is the most important determinant of your chances of success.

Conflicting perceptions are part of the natural order of things; part of the reason working out effective partnerships is so difficult. But if you don't look for agreement about *what* you are trying to achieve there is very little hope of agreeing *how* it should be achieved.

Consider two people in a room arguing about whether the window should be open or shut. There is no possible resolution of the conflict unless they agree what each is trying to achieve. Let us say 'fresh air' on the one hand (open) and 'prevention of cold/draught' on the other (closed). They can then seek a means of meeting both needs, at least partially, by alternative approaches or compromise. But the argument about the window can never be resolved. It is either open or shut. Partnership is often constrained by 'window' issues. The way to deal with them is to refer back to first principles and primary objectives; to look for other ways to address a problem.

Part Three

It is important to get the principles right but some clichés express a truth: the devil is indeed in the detail. In Part Three I consider the generic management and planning issues. You will need to extrapolate some of these using your knowledge of the special issues concerned with the particular target group of consumers, the different personalities involved in the partnership, the individual trajectory it has followed, its history, its politics and the current pressures which are being applied to it. I have done my best to infer what these might be from my own experience and I have suggested some further sources. But all partnerships are individual, so generic principles carry you just so far and no farther!

My intention is at least to give you as comprehensive an agenda as possible of issues to address and a commentary about some things I know have worked in the past and some things I know definitely do not work.

Because it is concerned with the practical world of 'how to' I suspect that for most people it will be most useful to read the book as a series of reference sections, as and when issues arise to be addressed. Each of the headings is covered, even if only in a paragraph or two, in the next chapter, so if you read that you start with the outline into which you can begin to paint your own colours as things develop.

In the final chapter I have tried to pull together the really critical issues which make or break successful partnerships. I have also tried to identify some of the factors which are likely to influence the way they will unfold in the future.

CHAPTER I

Partnership: The Agenda

Figure 1.1 illustrates the main items on the partnership agenda and their principal relationships. Throughout the book you will find similar maps focusing in more detail on the issues to be dealt with. This is, if you like, the large-scale map to which they all relate. Let us consider the five main headings in this figure – these correspond to the five themes in the book. The first four headings are much the same as the four chapter headings in Part Two; the fifth, 'Managing change', corresponds to the two first chapters of Part Three.

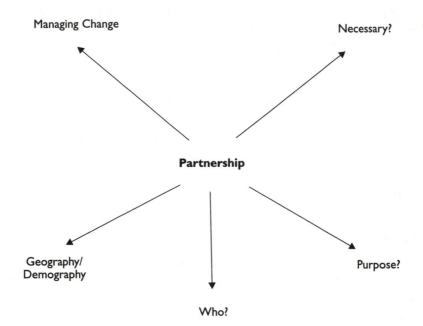

Figure 1.1 The main items on the partnership agenda

IS THIS PARTNERSHIP NECESSARY?

Definitions

Some so-called partnerships are definitely not necessary as they are, because they have become historical relics with little of their original purpose. Typically events have moved on but the meeting habit remains! Historical relics apart, the first step in dealing with the question is to define what sort of partnership you have at the moment and what sort you want in the future.

For the purposes of this book I have defined the word 'partnership' in the broadest possible terms. You will find more discussion of the definition in Chapter 2 but the general sense in which I have used it corresponds with my opening statement that this book is concerned with 'the effective co-ordination of public sector and voluntary effort which is intended to benefit people who are in need'.

Within that broad frame there are several different kinds of partnership corresponding to different purposes. They include partnerships for the collaboration of effort, commissioning of services, and consultation with, or the participation of, service users. Some partnerships are formed for the purpose of joint planning of a specific range of services but (more frequently, recently) broad-based strategic forums have been created to co-ordinate a wide range of collaborative effort.

For some specialist services some areas have opted to set up full joint management of a combined service. The most frequent examples of this are perhaps the Children and Adolescent Mental Health Services (CAMHS) combining psychiatry, psychology, education and social work. If you are planning a joint service of some kind in your area, have a look at your local CAMHS. It might provide you with some useful insights into what you should pursue and what to avoid.

Finally there are joint projects, focused on a specific task and usually time-limited. They can arise from a strategic forum initiative or from a less formal collaboration and they usually cease once the purpose is achieved (or abandoned).

Context

The context in which the partnership exists is all-important and it covers a range of factors including the financial and legal framework, the people involved, the driving factors (see below), local political and administrative history, the amount of pressure on the services, the local balance of power and influence and, not least, the target user group and degree of specialisation of the range of services.

Taken together, the contextual factors and the way to manage them are the subject of this book. They will determine what type of partnership is necessary and possible. Certain projects demand a certain type of partnership (which we will discuss in more detail later). But there is no avoiding the fact that other contextual factors may make it impossible or at least unwise to pursue the 'ideal' model immediately. For example, joint management requires clear leadership and accountability for success. If two people or two institutions are fighting like rats in a sack to gain primary control, it can be positively dangerous and damaging to the services to establish a joint management arrangement before the issue is substantively resolved.

The drivers

The primary drivers which have brought the partnership into existence and continue to sustain it are sufficiently important to consider separately. The lowest common denominator may sometimes be the existence of a powerful external driver which sustains the partnership without regard to the wishes of its internal members. There are four kinds of driver: legal obligation, statutory guidance, funding and better outcomes and value.

Legal obligation

Sometimes the law sets out, more or less explicitly, a duty to act in a way which falls within our definition of partnership. The multidisciplinary Youth Offending Teams (YOTs) were established in just this way. The Crime and Disorder Act 1998, section 39, says unequivocally:

Youth offending teams

39. – (1) Subject to subsection (2) below, it shall be the duty of each local authority, acting in co-operation with the persons and bodies mentioned in subsection (3) below, to establish for their area one or more youth offending teams.

More recently the Children Act 2004 establishes:

- a duty on Local Authorities to make arrangements to promote co-operation between agencies and other appropriate bodies (such as voluntary and community organisations) in order to improve children's well-being...and a duty on key partners to take part in the co-operation arrangements;
- a duty on key agencies to safeguard and promote the welfare of children; etc.

The means are less explicit than in the previous case but the demand for action is just as definite.

Statutory guidance

Many of the same considerations apply to government guidance. The distinction between legislation (Acts of Parliament and Statutory Instruments allowed by an Act) and guidance (government letters of guidance sent to local and other public authorities) is more to do with language and culture than impact. 'Guidance' is expressed in non-legal language but the word is really a throwback, a misnomer. 'Instruction' would describe the impact better. Several matters of guidance have been tested in the High Court and the ruling has always been that the Secretary of State and his officials can, in effect, order local authorities, for example, to act as they see fit. Once those orders are expressed formally in a letter of guidance they become, for all practical purposes, law.

Take as an example the *National Service Framework for Older People* (Department of Health 2001). In April 2004 the director of care services at the Department of Health wrote to the English local authorities. The letter began as follows:

> Dear Colleague
>
> You will be aware that a key milestone in the National Service Framework for Older People has been reached. From 1 April 2004, the systems and processes needed to underpin the Single Assessment Process need to be in place in local health and social care systems. A summary of what should be in place from April 2004 is attached as an Annex.

Not much doubt there: it's an instruction, even though described as guidance.

Funding requirement

Both the Home Administrations and the European Union use targeted 'hypothecated' finance to promote social policy objectives. For perfectly valid reasons a multi-agency, multifaceted, collaborative approach is usually a requirement.

It is not unusual for partnerships to be established specifically in order to construct a credible bid. When partnerships are created specifically to secure funding it can consume all their energy. Sometimes everything goes into making the bid and very little goes into planning how the money will be used once it has been secured. It is, of course, vital that equal effort goes into planning the follow-through if the funding bid is successful.

Better outcomes and value

Better outcomes and value is the ultimate justification for all public sector partnerships and the reason that governments promote them. Many small, local collaborations begun by committed practitioners start with this as their primary, even their only, motive. Sadly it must be acknowledged that formal strategic partnerships seldom begin like this: outside forces more often push them into existence. Under these circumstances it is even more important for them to identify and describe a better outcomes/value purpose early in their life. Maintaining a function solely because someone else says you must isn't conducive to a good result!

WHAT IS ITS PURPOSE?

Early steps towards partnership tend to be characterised by a haystack of an agenda in search of purpose while the members try to clarify what they hope to achieve. This early churning process may well be necessary, especially if there is a weak tradition of collaboration. But the sooner the partnership can achieve unity of purpose, the better. A robust agreement about what the partnership is actually for is probably the most important thing of all.

A vision

The vision expresses the kind of world we wish to see; it's that simple. At least, it is until we have to agree a common statement with someone else. Consider a mental health partnership by way of illustration:

> The vision might be a world in which everyone is in good mental health. But what does it mean? It doesn't mean a stress-free world surely: stress is a part of the human condition and drives us forward to achieve new things. Does it mean free from mental illness which has an organic basis? Leaving aside the problems of defining 'organic' presumably we would not wish to exclude those whose mental health had been affected by serious emotional trauma. So just what does the first sentence mean?

As we are never going to get there, why bother with this ideal model? Because it is important to know where we are trying to get to. People with very different visions in their minds can rub along pragmatically and achieve good things. But the public has a right to know, and all stakeholders the right to participate in defining, what the partnership that has been established to provide them with a better service is trying to achieve.

The mission

The mission represents the rôle we see ourselves playing to realise the vision. The partnership comprises agencies which have different missions. In the mental health field psychiatrists, psychologists, nurses, social workers and therapists occupy different niches. How do we express the mission of the whole partnership? Let's continue our previous illustration:

> The partners start with 'to improve the quality of life of people suffering from a mental illness'. They will need to find a way of encompassing cure, support and palliative care. Having agreed how to express these purposes together, they face a new range of definition problems. Does the partnership accept a rôle in prevention? It may not be the specific job of any participating agency but can it be excluded? The NHS has often been criticised as 'the National Sickness Service' in the past. Is the partnership prepared to leave the challenge unmet in the face of higher priorities or stronger imperatives?

The strategy

People sometimes get into terrible knots over the meaning of words like 'strategy' and the difference between that and, for example, a 'plan'. The *Oxford Reference Dictionary* defines (non-military) strategy as 'a plan of action for business or politics', so the struggle is nugatory! Not all plans are strategies but all strategies are, or should be, plans. You don't need a strategy to take the kids to the beach for the day, but you would be wise to have a plan.

The use of the word 'strategy' implies a written statement of an agreed plan of action over a significant period of time to deliver usually multiple objectives. We will explore the development of a strategy in the context of partnership in Chapter 3. For the moment it is necessary to note that it must have as a minimum the following elements:

- future aspirations for the services (in this case all those provided by the partnership) and assumed benefits for users and carers
- current service provision – benefits, costs and shortcomings
- demographic information – needs and numbers
- objectives – and time, funds, leadership and evaluation to achieve them
- priorities, costs and savings
- commitments from each partner.

There are great benefits to be derived from finding ways to involve users and carers in developing the strategy from the beginning, though it is not necessarily easy to do. Professional priorities are seldom the same as those of users and carers. If the two latter are not taken into account as the strategy is developed, it is in danger of becoming flawed from the outset. The apparently faster pace of development if they are not involved is an illusion.

Management/delivery

Each of the constituent agencies likely to be involved in a partnership has been constituted to manage a different set of objectives from all the others. A partnership set up to meet the needs of elderly people may comprise one team responsible for nursing, another for geriatric medicine, another for social and residential care, another for housing and possibly another for social security. The needs of the whole person might be best identified, and responses initiated, by a 'one-stop shop', but only the partnership acting together could assume responsibility for setting that as a management objective because none of the members individually have that primary responsibility.

It takes vision to act together on a joint task which is no one agency's primary responsibility. In spite of the rhetoric, the statutory agencies in particular will not be judged primarily on their partnership efforts but on their achievement of various statutory targets. To be sure, multi-agency collaboration is now a target in itself and there is growing recognition that individual service objectives are more effectively realised in collaboration than in isolation. Nevertheless, strategic multi-agency priorities do have to compete with single-agency priorities for attention and resources and it is sensible to recognise when they might be in conflict.

WHO IS INVOLVED?

Self-evidently the people who are involved in a partnership constitute its potential strength or its weakness more than anything else. Who are the intended beneficiaries and how are they involved in the process and consulted about desired outcomes? Who is going to provide the necessary resources to implement the strategy and make the commitment to see it delivered? What rights do the various actors have and what responsibilities have they accepted or had imposed upon them?

I have explored this in a little more detail in Chapter 4 but understanding and managing corporate behaviour, negotiation, leadership and motivation are well beyond the scope of a short book on partnership. There are a few suggestions for further reading in the bibliography (e.g. Audit Commission 1998; Fisher and Ury 1982; Harrison *et al.* 2003; Pratt *et al.* 1999; Surowiecki 2004).

WHERE WILL IT SERVE?

In many cases this is not really an issue. A social work team working with a GP practice may well cover the same community. A strategic, borough-wide partnership including many local agencies working in the same borough will have no difficulty in answering the question. But the problem arises among partners whose boundaries are not co-terminous. For example, one CAMHS I know covers five different metropolitan boroughs. You can imagine the difficulties they face in trying to deliver an equitable service across five politically independent authorities with very different ideas about quality, standards and accountability.

Some of the issues which arise about demographic and geographic targeting are very specific to the particular situation but there are some generic issues to be faced whenever the problem arises. I discuss some of the common ones in Chapter 5.

HOW WILL IT WORK?

Issues of partnership management are covered in the first two chapters in Part Three. They deal with structure and authority, accountability, reporting and staffing issues, information and evaluation and timing and service delivery.

The general principle is that, however well intentioned the strategic purpose, a partnership can suffer and even fail on the detail. A successful partnership is well conceived and planned – and to work effectively it is also well managed.

PART TWO

The Strategic Issues

CHAPTER 2

Is this Partnership Necessary?

INTRODUCTION

The democratic participation of many people in governance usually leads to a better result in the end, but there is no denying that it is slower, more complex, more stressful, and consumes additional resources to make the process work. So it had better be necessary in the first place. It is sometimes assumed that it is better to have one or two people design something than many. 'A camel is a horse designed by a committee,' says the aphorism. But the evidence, at least as far as political and social structures are concerned, demonstrates the opposite. It may be more difficult to reach an acceptable solution openly and by engaging diversity, but the result is better.

In this chapter we explore two issues:

1. Given the nature of the tasks we are usually addressing in governance, some form of partnership is usually necessary or beneficial – but it isn't always so. There are some tasks which are best dealt with unilaterally. The potential partners should always be clear why a partnership approach is preferable in any particular case.

2. The word 'partnership' has come to cover a great many forms of collaboration. It is important to be clear not only that partnership is necessary, but what form it should take for a particular purpose.

The key components of the chapter are illustrated in Figure 2.1.

DEFINITIONS

'Partnership', like 'community' before it, has become one of those factotum words. Any two or more people living together, working together, sailing together, dancing together, even lunching together, is a partnership. By

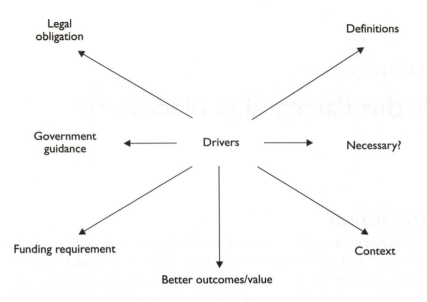

Figure 2.1 The determinants of necessary partnership

common assumption it's always a good thing: the Savlon of governance. Rub a little partnership on the problem and it will get better.

The first definition of 'partner' in the *Oxford English Dictionary* is 'a person who shares or takes part with another or others…with shared risks and profits'. But it certainly doesn't mean anything as committed as that in most government circulars and publications on the subject. In different contexts partnership can mean any of the following.

- **Collaboration** – ad hoc collaboration in the way agencies, teams or individual practitioners address a particular issue.

- **Consultation and participation** – engagement of service users and others in the process of redesign or in critical analysis of the way things have been done, with an eye to change.

- **Commissioning** – 'partnership' between service providers, especially voluntary bodies, and commissioners, especially public bodies.

- **Joint planning** – some shared planning from a plan worked out jointly to an exchange of draft plans to seek comments from the other agency(s) before final conclusions are reached.

- **Strategic forum** – a strategic forum of significant stakeholder agencies in the outcome of a major issue (for example, a range of services for one user group such as children or people suffering from mental illness).

- **Joint management** – the joint management of a range of services with shared objectives, costs, risks and benefits.

All these meanings are included in the word 'partnership' in the title of this book. They are all useful processes in different contexts, but immediately it is clear that the terms describe very different things.

Note that the six different meanings of partnership described above are not mutually exclusive. *Collaboration, commissioning* and *consultation and partici-pation* are free-standing. Each of them can take place independently of the others. But *collaboration* and *consultation and participation* are necessary components of any *strategic forum* or *joint planning* worthy of the name. Joint planning can take place independently. But a strategic forum is pretty mean-ingless if it doesn't lead to a joint plan. Finally, all other types of partnership need to be present as components of *joint management.* Figure 2.2 shows this rather complex set of relationships graphically.

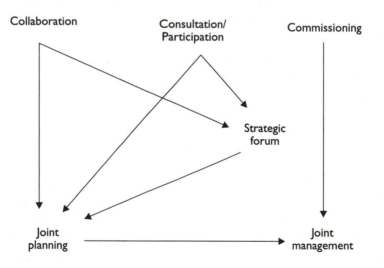

Figure 2.2 Different kinds of partnership

The following example illustrates the evolution of one kind of partnership into another:

> A health visitor, a social worker and a teacher have agreed to work together with a child they are all attempting to help. They share information about what they are doing in relation to the child and why. They agree to co-ordinate the timing of their various interventions. They meet regularly to discuss progress as they each see it and they share their plans for future work.

The situation described is an example of active collaboration. In the best run agencies it is a hallmark of good practice and it goes on all the time, to excellent effect. I would go so far as to say that good professional practice is not possible without this kind of collaboration. The professionals are each pursuing their own agenda in the knowledge that they can do so more effectively in collaboration with others who are having an important impact on the user of their service. They are accountable for their own decisions within their own hierarchy and they are not sharing risk or agreeing a joint benefit.

> The three professionals and the child's parents are delighted with the success of their collaboration. They conclude that they could extend the learning to the benefit of many of the children in the school. Together with the school nurse they promote a parents board and write a business plan for a joint project based on the school and its children. They submit the plan to their respective agencies, each of which agrees to second them for two days a week to the project, which will be evaluated at the end of one year against criteria written into the plan.

The collaboration has become joint management. They have set up a project for which they are jointly accountable. I would have liked to see their business plan: what, for example, are the additional benefits they envisage accruing from this formal partnership that they were not able to achieve by collaboration alone?

There is a warm glow attached to the idea of partnership. It feels as if we are being co-operative and mutually supportive. But it can be extremely hard work, potentially stressful and very wasteful of resources, unless the degree and kind of partnership is understood and agreed by the participants to be right for the sort of outcome they are aiming for. A partnership should always be a means to an end. It is always worth asking the question, 'Will this lead to a better, more integrated service on the ground for the people who it aims to serve, or can we achieve the same or a better service by a different form of integration – a different form of partnership?'

Some form of partnership is almost always necessary, or at least beneficial, for planning and making policy changes. Any change contemplated by one stakeholder is almost certain to have consequences for the others. It's not just the users and carers who will be affected but all the other service providers and commissioners as well.

You may not consult your local supermarket about changes in your shopping patterns but they would very much like it if you did; and they spend large sums of money trying to anticipate those changes. They would, in short, like a partnership with you (in this case, of course, to the exclusion of other supermarkets).

On the other hand, many activities are better undertaken alone. If I go to my GP I don't want to find a social worker, a district nurse and a pharmacist sitting in on the session, even though I might subsequently need any or all of them.

The point is that questions about what should be done are almost inevitably better answered with the full engagement of all those who will be affected by the answer. But if the joint decision-making gets too far into the detail of *how* to do the business every decision becomes slow, inflexible, expensive and ultimately unresponsive. The service user must always be involved; anyone else only as needed.

It's not just direct services to the user which are affected by this. Many of us will have experienced small groups of senior managers who troop around to every meeting together, either for security or because they don't trust each other. If every corporate act of a partnership has to be played out in this way by all the partners, movement will be slow and cumbersome indeed.

CONTEXT

The decision about the best kind of partnership to go for depends on a large number of contextual conditions. Some of the more important of these are listed in Figure 2.3. In the broadest sense all the subjects covered in this book are part of the context. And once a change has begun to take place in response to a partnership it too becomes part of the new context.

I don't intend to go through each of the contextual headings, but let's consider two or three examples to illustrate the process of deciding what kind of partnership might be indicated under specific conditions.

History and politics

Nothing arrives from nowhere. Let us imagine a scenario in a local authority area with a history of insularity among the different agencies and local authority departments (and even divisions in some cases). They are characterised by a 'silo' approach to service planning and provision and mutual distrust among the agencies. In our example, government guidance and pressure has

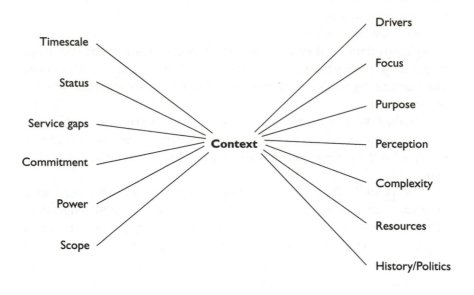

Figure 2.3 The all-important context

forced them to establish a strategic forum for children and (this is the new part) start taking it seriously and expecting results.

It would be a high-risk strategy, under those circumstances, to try to move straight into a comprehensive service management partnership regardless of the other contextual conditions. There is no track record of joint, or even shared, planning, and though there might be pockets of effective collaboration they have been essentially operational, set up as local good practice in spite of, rather than because of, the hitherto prevailing ethos among the agencies.

Timescale

In these changing times few partnerships (or anything else) justify the description 'permanent', but timescales vary widely.

- At the shortest end of the spectrum a key stakeholder in the process may be suffering from a hangover or a stomach ache or he may have just heard that his daughter has achieved a first-class honours degree. Such personal matters should not impinge on the governance of services – but they do!

- At the next level, a key short-term stage may receive, or fail to receive, the necessary funding to proceed. It's probably not make-or-break but it does need to be worked around.

- At a further stage, local political goodwill may shift in favour of or against the strategy favoured by the partnership.

- Finally, at the time of writing, we have a government actively pushing for the development of partnership and prepared to invest in it. The government looks politically secure, so the policy is unlikely to change in the short term. But don't forget that the financial climate might change nevertheless. The rhetoric might stay the same but the cash flow may not.

Power

Influence is a complex matter but it is idle, in all the talk about 'equal partners', to ignore the reality that some players have much greater power to influence the direction of change than others. 'The Pope? How many divisions has he got?' asked Stalin. In the context of local governance the question might be updated to 'Voluntary organisations? How many millions are they going to invest?' The big players are the local authority and the health service, because they are going to pay for any changes. To express the process from their perspective they have to justify to their constituencies the diversion of resources from existing priorities to this new way of doing things, while at the same time losing a degree of sovereign control.

Finally, in the background sit the government administrations with their power to set and enforce regulations and standards and their control over much the largest element of the local budgets across all the services. They may not be seen as part of the local partnership but their power over its deliberations is very great.

DRIVERS

There are four basic reasons why a public sector partnership of some kind might be formed or sustained. They are:

- legal obligation
- government guidance
- funding requirement
- better outcomes and value.

Of these, the first two are external necessities and the third a powerful external motivator; only the fourth is driven from within, often from or close to operational level, as in our preceding example. Of course, the first three are themselves initiated in the belief that they will result in better outcomes and value – but it is important to remember that not all the stakeholders necessarily start from this position.

A second issue of importance is that partnership, however extensive, will never obviate the need to collaborate outside it. You might, for example, decide to set up a partnership to provide services for people with a disability, but there will always be many services outside the partnership which are important to disabled people and with which a fit needs to be negotiated.

Legal obligation

The law is expressed in common law, which doesn't much concern us here, primary legislation (Acts of Parliament) and secondary legislation (Statutory Instruments allowed by an Act and laid before Parliament by the Secretary of State), and the exact meaning of the expression is interpreted by the high court. It is important to remember that until one party challenges another in court, claiming that they are acting unlawfully, everyone has an equal right to put their own interpretation on what the law means.

On the whole, when the law says there must be a partnership it does so by creating a body combining formerly separate services. The Youth Justice Board and the local youth offending teams provide a very clear example of this. The following extract from the Crime and Disorder Act 1998 sets out exactly what must be done.

> 39. – (1) Subject to subsection (2) below, it shall be the duty of each local authority, acting in co-operation with the persons and bodies mentioned in subsection (3) below, to establish for their area one or more youth offending teams.
>
> [...]
>
> (3)   It shall be the duty of –
>
>> (a) every chief officer of police any part of whose police area lies within the local authority's area; and
>>
>> (b) every probation committee or health authority any part of whose area lies within that area, to co-operate in the discharge by the local authority of their duty under subsection (1) above.
>
> (4)   The local authority and every person or body mentioned in subsection (3) above shall have power to make payments towards expenditure incurred by, or for purposes connected with, youth offending teams –

[...]

(5)   A youth offending team shall include at least one of each of the following, namely –

   (a) a probation officer;

   (b) a social worker of a local authority social services department;

   (c) a police officer;

   (d) a person nominated by a health authority any part of whose area lies within the local authority's area;

   (e) a person nominated by the chief education officer appointed by the local authority under section 532 of the Education Act 1996.

[...]

(7)   It shall be the duty of the youth offending team or teams established by a particular local authority [...] to co-ordinate the provision of youth justice services for all those in the authority's area who need them; [etc.]

The Children Act 2004, at least in the provisions related to England, sets up a partnership equally explicitly in the form of a children's trust.

Under these circumstances nobody is allowed to change the rules; the partners must simply get on with it and form the partnership body which the law demands.

Where the law creates an obligation without specifying the means, the results are less clear. The Children and Young Persons Act 1989, section 17, imposes a duty on the local authority (i.e. not just the social services department) to make provision for children in need. Some authorities have interpreted this for many years as a requirement for effective strategic collaboration at the least (such as shared planning arrangements and joint protocols). In a few cases they have been moving towards joint management. Much more recently, in anticipation of the requirements of the Children Act 2004, the majority have started down that path in relation to at least some of the services.

Government guidance

It is not always recognised that government guidance, i.e. letters and reports of guidance sent to local and other public authorities, has statutory force. This is guidance about what *must* be done rather than what might be done (if you feel like it). Local authorities in particular have been challenged in the courts on a number of occasions on the grounds that they are not carrying out government guidance. If the court finds the allegation to be true, they find against the authority.

In other words, the authority cannot mount a defence that they had a choice whether to follow the guidance or not. For example, the universally established area child protection committees are not 'statutory' bodies. They have not been described in law (though they are now, in the Children Act 2004, under their new name 'safeguarding children boards'); they are, however, described in the various editions of *Working Together to Safeguard Children*, government guidance with the effective force of law.

In Wales, where children's trusts are not a legal requirement, the Welsh Assembly has made it clear in guidance that the local authorities must maintain children's strategic forums to pursue a similar agenda to the trusts in England (though arguably there is more flexibility about exactly how they do it).

One big difference between statute law and guidance is the language used. Statutes are precise and prescriptive. Guidance is, for the most part, exhortative and more open to local interpretation. The other major difference is that guidance is focused on issues of often quite detailed policy and practice. It is, in short, much more about 'how to' than statute.

This is very significant in the context of partnership. Many circulars and guidance papers use the word 'partnership', but it is clear from the context that they do not necessarily prescribe the definition. In other words, it is down to local authorities to decide what will work best for them. Look at the summary of the Local Authority Social Services Letter in England, *Preparing Older People's Strategies* (LASSL (2003) 2: Department of Health 2003). The highlighting of phrases in bold type is mine.

i. This joint DH/ODPM circular **draws attention** to the document *Preparing Older People's Strategies* and **encourages its use** by PCTs and local social services authorities as part of drawing up Local Delivery Plans and capacity plans for older people's services which includes working **in partnership** with housing authorities.

ii. This circular will make clear that strategies **may be led by housing authorities or local councils corporately**, where that is agreed locally, with agreed proposals incorporated in NHS/social care plans.

iii. This circular stresses that older people's strategies incorporating the housing dimension, where this has not already been done, need to engage with, and consult older people fully, and proper time should be allowed for this.

The tone of this particular circular is rather more than usually permissive, but the loose use of the word 'partnership' and the implied 'Do it how you like, but do it!' are not unusual.

In fairness, governments in the UK tread a difficult line between prescription and permission. If they leave local agencies to work out their own salvation they stand accused of 'washing their hands' of problems. If they are highly prescriptive they are accused of control-freakery and of not understanding the problems of implementation on the ground.

Implications

Local stakeholders considering the implications of guidance should not read into it more than it implies. What are the *constraints* on their actions? Does the exhortation imply joint management, joint planning, or strategic form and does it allow you to choose what seems to work best? What *requirements* does it demand (in terms, for example, of reporting, benchmarks or targets)? Can *local views* of policy outcome be accommodated within the guidance; and how should implementation be adjusted to accommodate them?

That kind of thinking is useful to avoid being driven too far by government circular and reading more into it than is really there. But the existence of the guidance can be used to apply pressure to reluctant stakeholders who would prefer to continue doing things the old way in spite of a general view about the need to change. Government advice is driven by a commitment to improve quality. Though sometimes clumsy it is usually pushing in the direction of good professional practice and outcomes as the ultimate goal of collaboration and partnership. That is not to imply that the intention is necessarily achieved by every initiative!

Funding requirement

The European Union and UK governments use targeted finance to encourage local authorities and others to pursue their favoured social policy objectives. On a different scale the Lottery Fund 'for good causes' and charitable funding bodies also do this. Almost all of them want to see evidence of purpose and chances of success. The great majority also want to see evidence of 'partnership' in preparing the bid. Indeed, partnerships are often established specifically to enter the bidding process.

The driving force in these partnerships is sometimes collaboration in order to attract the money, rather than collaboration in order to pursue the objectives, whatever they are. The big danger in this is that if the funding is the primary objective, little attention is paid to the secondary objective: how to use it when you get it. One might imagine that the funding bodies, whether they be government, local authorities or charitable funds, should be able to spot this in the way the applications are framed but the fact is that they often don't.

Sometimes, especially in the case of large funded EU or government projects, an elaborate cross agency process is set up to monitor or control the use of the resource. The European Union Objective 1 fund for social regeneration in deprived areas, for example, generated such groups wherever the fund operates. Such groups are inevitably known as 'partnerships'. Look at the following example:

The South Yorkshire vision and ambition (for Objective 1)

Even before it was apparent that South Yorkshire would qualify for Objective 1 status, the South Yorkshire Forum (representing the public, private and community and voluntary sectors across the area) began work on developing a new vision for South Yorkshire. The Forum's aim was to agree a clear and achievable aspiration to which public policy and private sector support could be harnessed. The partnership developed and adopted *Making the Breakthrough*, a strategic framework for the achievement of a transformational change in the area's prospects, designed to drive the direction of all sources of regeneration funding and not just those coming from Europe.

The South Yorkshire Forum is a top level partnership body comprising all the main players in the economic regeneration of the area. It is chaired by the private sector and has had overall responsibility for receiving progress reports and ratifying decisions.

More recently, it is from the South Yorkshire Forum that membership of the Programme Monitoring Committee (PMC) has emerged. While the PMC will now take over the task of steering the Objective 1 programme, the South Yorkshire Forum will be responsible for the development of a comprehensive and commonly owned strategy to revitalise the area's economy.

(South Yorkshire Forum 2000. Reproduced with permission.)

This is clearly a strategic forum. Equally clearly, it was set up to deal with the inflow of finance. The 'new vision' was originally expressed in those terms. Only later did it acquire the 'development of a comprehensive and commonly owned strategy to revitalise the area's economy'. It looks as though the forum was set up to spend the money and only later did it begin to work out what to spend the money on.

This might sound unduly pedantic. After all, we might use slightly different words but we all agree broadly what the objective is, don't we? Well, no, not necessarily. On a very different scale from the above example, part of the Millennium funding was earmarked in Wales to provide capital funding for new village halls. Some of the bids came from community groups which had been trying for years to get a building established or refurbished. Others came from groups established specifically to take advantage of the fund. Many in the latter category had very different ideas about what their hall should be for once it was built – a rich source of community conflict for the future!

Better outcomes and value

Top level formal partnerships seldom start from this baseline but many informal partnerships, often between concerned professionals, anxious to improve the quality of what they do for those to whom they provide a service, have better outcomes and value as their central objective. They are often not well supported by their parent agencies and not integrated into the more formal 'strategic' partnerships which exist further up the food chain.

Better outcomes and value is the ultimate justification for all public sector partnerships, so it is unfortunate that those which have been established for exactly this purpose are often poorly exploited. Practitioners need to be more reflective about the significance of what they are doing for their own small groups of users for the wider world and more assertive in demanding better strategic support. Senior managers trying to develop a more integrated approach among their services need to discover what exists already and use it as a platform on which to build.

CHAPTER 3

The Purposes of Partnership

INTRODUCTION

The starting point for many partnerships is outside pressure, so, for the partners, the initial purpose is to demonstrate that the partnership exists! The Government, the council, the chief executive or someone with the power to decide has indeed decided, so a large group of senior executives representing the various 'partners' assembles under the appropriate name and discusses a large and disjointed agenda. Action points usually amount to the construction of more agenda items for the future and information to illuminate those already tabled. This process can continue for a long time until someone with sufficient authority tries to break the logjam.

Often such a starting point is a necessary first step and sometimes, especially in a locality where there is a weak tradition of collaboration, a further period of 'churning' is inevitable while people gain the confidence to enable them to say dangerous and challenging things. But this opening phase should end as soon as possible. It does fulfil its initial purpose of enabling people to learn about each other, but it is an expensive device. A typical group of perhaps 25 senior representative staff costs, conservatively, £3000 per meeting by the time additionals have been added. It appears on the budget of none of the agencies represented, of course, but it represents a significant opportunity cost for all of them: while they are sitting round the meeting table they are not doing the other things for which they are paid.

Much worse than the cost, however, is the blight which such bodies can cause. More informal and more output-directed efforts to develop partnership approaches are often stalled because 'We must refer this to the partnership board so that it can be properly integrated'. Integrated with what?

The way forward from this position is to agree a statement of purpose. What does the partnership intend to do? What does it define as its remit? What does it intend to change? How will it affect people and services and how will it engage the active participation of service users and carers? This process and the developments which flow from it are the focus of this chapter.

When you are developing a partnership the sine qua non is acceptability. The sum may be greater than the parts, but that is not where you start: every key player must sign up to a starting position which goes at least some of the way towards what they want encompassed.

The components of the process of identifying and delivering the purpose is illustrated in Figure 3.1.

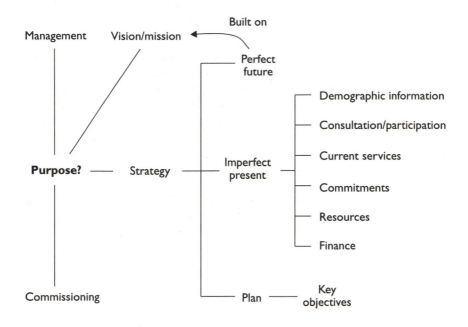

Figure 3.1 Identifying the purpose of a partnership

VISION AND MISSION

Many people are cynical and dismissive about mission statements and regard them as airy-fairy waffle which has nothing to do with the 'real business of the organisation'. Sometimes, no doubt, that is exactly what they are. But an organisation without a clear sense of purpose, a vision of what it exists to deliver, has no foundation. Where there is a collective of more than one organisation it is more important than ever to work out exactly what they have joined forces to achieve.

There is often a starting assumption among some of the partners that everyone around the table shares the same goals and values. There may still be others precious enough to believe that those round the table cannot possibly understand their goals and values because they have not had the necessary training and experience. The process of seeking to agree a statement about the fundamental reason the partnership exists undermines both these positions. Different starting points soon emerge and professional obfuscation is challenged as part of the process.

> The process was graphically illustrated by an aspiring management partnership for children's services some years ago. They had been through the churning stage for almost a year and had accumulated an agenda and supporting papers the size of a small haystack. It became clear to them that they were lost and they invited me to help them do some 'blue sky thinking' about where they were going.
>
> The first stage of the two-day seminar for that purpose focused on agreeing what they thought the partnership was for. Perhaps the most important debate was about the target group and how to define them. We discussed 'vulnerable children', 'children at risk' and 'children in need', but finally agreed (this was some years before the government Green Paper *Every Child Matters*: Department for Education and Skills 2003) that these were priorities still to be decided. The partnership existed to serve all the children in the community. The various attempts to describe a target group had been bureaucratic, agency limits. The whole group perspective enabled a rethink towards establishing priorities in accordance with the needs of children rather than the obligations of the agencies. It was a critical decision; it formed a baseline for everything that followed.

It is not difficult to draft a statement of purpose. Any competent and thoughtful member of the partnership can do it. The key stage is to get each of the partners and the service users to examine it critically and, if necessary, modify it – preferably together. The process may reveal considerable tensions, or it may be very easy. But in the end the final draft should be an expression of what all the stakeholders want the partnership to be about.

The vision

The vision is an attempt to describe the sort of society we wish to promote or support, relevant to the aims of the partnership. It is always at a huge level of generalisation because it needs to encompass a broad range of often competing perceptions. If you ask, for example, what sort of ideal society older people would aspire to live in, you will get perhaps half a dozen broad clusters of ideas of what the ideal world should be like. The problem is that some of them will be mutually incompatible. Democracy is intended to allow these competing visions enough expression and enough hope for the future to stop their advocates attacking each other physically: 'This may not be the sort of society I want but at least I can vote against it with some hope of a change.' The partnership must be careful to frame its vision in a way which will be seen by service users and others as non-partisan.

In theory that might lead to something anodyne and blandly meaningless, but in practice that doesn't usually happen. Within all these competing world views there will be many common themes. Many of them will equate roughly to Maslow's 'hierarchy of needs'. They will almost all want:

- good health and health care
- sufficient income to live on comfortably and securely into the future
- security and safety at home and outside
- attention and respect from younger people
- as much personal independence as circumstances will allow (access, transport, information).

Many of them will want:

- opportunities for stimulation and new learning
- a relevant social and economic rôle in the community
- to be cared about and care for others.

The vision will describe the kind of society which will promote these aspirations. The services within the purview of the partnership will never be able to deliver such a society, which will in any case depend on more things than services. But everything it does should contribute in some way to their realisation. It should always be legitimate to ask, 'In what way will this course of action contribute to our stated vision?'

At risk of repetition, it is vital that the broadest possible range of stakeholders be involved in describing and endorsing the vision. If the potential service users don't share your vision of what their world should be like, they will not allow you to achieve it. If the politicians are not on board, they will frustrate the development as soon as it becomes difficult or expensive.

The mission

If the vision is a house, the mission of the building firm is to build it. The mission of the bricklayer is to lay the bricks. 'Mission' means 'job', or perhaps 'job done by important people'! It is the answer to the question, 'What part do we play in helping [the target of our efforts] to get closer to her vision of where she wants to go?'

Describing the mission is much more problematic at strategic, multi-agency level than it is at operational level. Practitioners might ask, 'How do we collaborate effectively to provide the best possible combination of services for this particular user?' It might be technically difficult to achieve but at least you know exactly what they are trying to do. But when 'the service user' is an amorphous demographic potential and you know that you are going to have to select priorities to narrow the potential users down to actual beneficiaries, it is far from easy to get it right.

It is nevertheless important to describe the job that has been set for the partnership. Without that core description the debate will range between saving the world and doing nothing, and it will be impossible to set priorities and objectives. Some of the issues are illustrated in the following example:

> A strategic partnership is trying to identify its mission. There is a well established link between poorer health, poorer social position and poorer educational outcomes on the one hand, and poverty and poor housing on the other. But the latter two areas are outside the core business of any of the partners.
>
> As a result of the debate the partnership recognises that much of its effort will be marginalised if it simply ignores these two key factors, so it decides to take them on as part of the mission. They see absence of the housing directorate as a major weakness of the existing partnership and decide to invite them to participate as the agency best placed to address this major component of disadvantage.
>
> Poverty and social exclusion are more difficult. They might invite the local social exclusion unit to join the partnership but, having looked at its remit, they decide against that course. The bigger the partnership, the more diffuse its impact. But they must address the issue – otherwise, to include those factors in the mission is meaningless grandstanding: words leading nowhere.
>
> In the event, they do include it, and subsequently commission a project to identify the demographics of local child poverty and the key players, public, voluntary and commercial, with which they need to engage in dialogue to identify joint action.

The salient point to bear in mind from this illustration is that if the partnership had simply 'got on with the job' without considering what the job was, this potentially critical initiative would never have happened.

STRATEGY

A strategy is simply a long-term plan which aims to be as comprehensive as possible within the timescale, and with available resources and information. All strategies need to relate to other significant plans and strategies which have an influence on them and which they will influence.* That is not easy to achieve. At one stage there were so many plans and initiatives emerging from Whitehall, each usually supported by a funding stream, that it was almost impossible to keep track of them. Most of them exhorted, and purported to reward, 'joined-up governance', but they didn't represent the concept in action very well themselves! The problem still exists, but the Government has listened to complaints of this nature and makes more effort to connect its own initiatives as part of its advice.

> * But they often don't relate. One of the authorities I worked with as a member of a performance action team had a plethora of plans, strategies, policies and initiatives. Whatever the subject or the range of services, there was some policy statement or plan in existence. The trouble with them was that they seldom bore any relationship to each other. Some of them were very thoughtful and well worked out, but they might as well have existed at the bottom of a well for all the impact they had on the real world.

In essence a strategy should have three components:

- a vision of the perfect future
- information about the imperfect present
- a plan for travelling from one to the other.

It's important that they should be developed in that sequence; see Figure 3.2.

If you start with the question 'Where am I now?', two things happen. First, the question is almost boundless: 'Where am I now in relation to what?' Any journey needs a reference point. Second, the limitations of the current position become the starting point for the imagination about what is possible and what is desirable. To illustrate this, consider a strategy for residential care for elderly people:

> If we start with 'Where are we now?' we count how many elderly people are in residential and other care now; how the number has changed over the past X period; how much this costs; how dependent they are; how many staff are involved, and so on and so on. I could easily fill this book with the list of possible questions to ask. But we have not considered yet what any of this is for and what we are trying to achieve.
>
> Now we consider the future. We know how many we are caring for today, but how many should we be aiming to care for next year, where, in what circumstances, at what cost and so on? Each of these questions is predicted, unless we consciously avoid it, by the 'Where are we now?' questions. We need to consider why we are providing residential care; what other options there are; what would be the ideal result. None of those questions is illuminated in the slightest by reference to the present situation, but they might well be clouded by it.

Just before we begin to consider the three elements of a strategy, a word about definitions, in particular the word 'objective', around which there is some confusion. It is defined in the *Oxford English Dictionary* as 'something sought or aimed at'. Within management and government circles the word has tended to acquire some additional tags including the 'SMART' acronym (simple, measurable, achievable, realistic, time specified). We need the words to describe a process which begins with a *vision* and a *mission*, which we have already dealt with, and goes on to elaborate the mission into a small number of key *objectives*, all of which must be aimed at in order to achieve the vision. I could use the word 'aims' to designate these, but the word feels rather woolly these days and that is the last thing I wish to convey.

Rather than make elaborate distinctions between strategic objectives and management objectives, which need to be 'smart', I have used the rather jargony word 'deliverables'. There is no such noun in the *Oxford English Dictionary*, but the meaning extrapolated from the adjective is 'things which are rendered'. They are to be not merely aimed at, but to be produced.

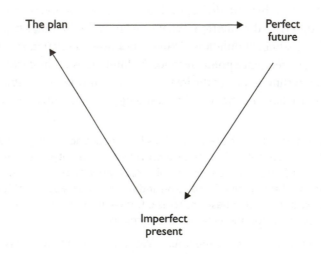

Figure 3.2 The basic planning cycle

The perfect future

The vision and mission describe the desired future in broad terms. They provide a direction of travel. Even for a loose collaborative partnership it is worth the time and effort required to negotiate five or six key objectives which resonate with users and which engage the active consent of the other significant stakeholders. They should start from the question 'What kind of services should we be providing?', not 'How can we develop what we have?'

As a facilitator helping to develop partnership projects I have found it useful to start by demanding the best that people can imagine. Anything is allowed except comments which begin 'We can't do that because...'. From a long list of perhaps twenty or more possibilities the process of reduction begins. Surprisingly, it is usually possible to create a shortlist of five or six (the number is agreed beforehand) without substantial loss. And it is important to do so. A short list of key objectives is enough to relate the whole of the partnership's business to. A large number simply becomes confusing. A partnership contains many complexities and ambiguities to be managed. The root purpose of all its effort should be expressed as simply and clearly as possible.

One of the great virtues of the Green Paper *Every Child Matters* (Department for Education and Skills 2003), which led to the Children Act 2004, was that it sought to address five simple goals (objectives in the sense used above). Its purpose for children was that:

- they should be healthy
- they should be safe and secure
- they should achieve their potential and enjoy doing so
- they should contribute to society
- they should achieve socio-economic success.

For all the complexity and creative thinking that would be required to deliver it, the purpose itself was clear, simple and explicit.

The final thing to say about these key objectives is that they should make sense!

- They should be expressed in language which is understandable by politicians and public, users and carers.
- They should be capable of achievement and evaluation. Nothing wrong with aspirational language, 'All older people should be able to maintain independence...', but it should be capable of comparison. How much more independence, among how many people, have we been able to create since we stated this objective?
- They should be realistic. I once asked a wise colleague what she thought of a new health plan which had just been published. 'It's wonderful,' she replied. 'If this plan is properly implemented nobody in the region will ever die again.'

The imperfect present

The next stage of strategy development is to assemble information and analyse it in relation to desired goals. In some ways life has become much simpler since the advent of the computer as the standard business tool. Access to information is a great deal easier and much more of it is recorded automatically for one purpose, yet available for quite another. But information collected for one purpose doesn't necessarily read across to another, as the difficulties encountered by agency partners when they attempt to integrate their databases for the first time always show. And even if it did, we still have to decide what information we need for what purpose. The following are the key sources.

Demographic information

A needs analysis based on the profile of the area population is a must. Without it the partnership can't decide the scale of the services it needs to commission, where they should be located and what particular needs they should target.

Consultation and participation

The most important stakeholders in the process have an important rôle in commenting on what exists, none more so than the users of the services and their carers. Their perspective on the effectiveness of what is done is critical.

Current services

Clearly a good description of current services (where they are, what they are for, what they actually do, how much they cost, how they are commissioned, how they are evaluated, how they are changing) is essential information in preparing to plan for the future.

Commitments

Everyone has commitments, legal, financial and professional, which carry forward beyond the immediate present. How long is a significant hypothecated government grant on which this range of services depends committed for? How long is this agency committed to maintain a seconded member of staff to this partnership? What other projects exist (outside the scope of the partnership) which might make inroads into the agency's ability to manoeuvre, and how long is the commitment?

Resources

There may be a joint commitment to a shared objective, but how much of the total resource pool directed to the purposes of the partnership is also pooled for the purpose of planning the future? Can money be moved around in practice if to do so will lead to a better service? Can it be moved across from one agency to another or dedicated to partnership management, if it is that kind of partnership?

Finance

The practicalities of financial decision-making and management vary considerably from one agency to another. An important platform for a joint plan is to understand how those processes work and produce results in each of the major funding agencies. Are there possible conflicts? Are there different timescales? Is there a different (possibly conflicting) consultation and negotiation process?

The plan

Now the partnership knows what it wants to do, what it is doing at the moment, and some of the constraints on its immediate ability to manoeuvre, it has enough information to build a plan (or a strategy if you prefer, or even a strategic plan!).

A plan is more than merely aspirational – it is, or should be, a realistic statement of intended delivery, so the first question is what is the best way to achieve it. At this point there are several choices that partnership members can make, largely depending on what type of partnership it is:

1. The partnership or its planning team can stay together and produce a completely joint plan.

2. The planning team can work together but on separate plans for (some or all of) the partners.

3. The individual partners can go it alone. Each of them develops their own plan to contribute to the objectives and keeps the others advised at intervals to be agreed.

In making that decision for year one it is worth remembering that it is not set in stone. There may be all sorts of practical, historical and personality reasons for aiming for an interim stage in year one with the intention, if the plan(s) work, to take a further step the following year, and maybe yet another step in year three.

Some of the more significant indicators for greater or lesser integration of planning are as follows:

- Different agencies in the partnership may collect their planning information in different ways (though the more quickly they can begin to share a common dataset the better).
- There may be a history of uneasy relationships in the past among some of the agencies.
- The huge amount of mutual learning to be gained from sharing information during joint planning may justify the effort even in the face of other difficulties.

However it is done, the plan(s) must:

- work within a specified *timescale*
- clearly and simply describe a set of *deliverables* which together move forward all the key objectives
- describe *priorities* in time and importance
- identify the *resources* needed to deliver, both practical and financial
- show how *change* will be managed and controlled
- describe *evaluation* criteria and method(s).

In other words, in that overworked management cliché already referred to, the plans must be:

- **S**imple
- **M**easurable
- **A**chievable
- **R**ealistic
- **T**imely.

COMMISSIONING

This is the process of turning resources into a suitable range of services, or of changing an unsuitable range into something better. Within a partnership there are likely to be very different traditions about in-house services, service level agreements, voluntary partnerships, contracts with suppliers and other means of getting things done. Whether the plan contains a section on how the services it proposes to change are to be commissioned or there is a separate commissioning strategy, the two things are intimately connected. No commissioning strategy is possible without a statement in substantial detail about service intentions and the resources to support them.

In 2004 I was a member of a team from KPMG Consultants working with a local authority to develop a children's services commissioning strategy. Our report contained the illustration shown in Figure 3.3.

The illustration neatly encapsulates the commissioning process required to deliver any group of services.

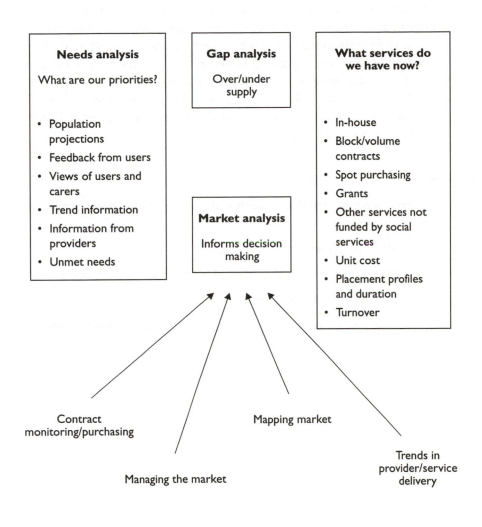

Figure 3.3 The commissioning process

MANAGEMENT

Part Three of this book deals in more detail with management issues in general. The point of including this heading here is to emphasise that form should follow function. First you decide what you want to do, then you decide what sort of organisation you need to do it. The structural and management question is, 'What is the best way to deliver the objectives the partnership has set for itself?' There is no purpose, for example, in seconding a co-ordinator or a group of staff to serve a strategic forum unless they have an explicit purpose which is not being met by staff from the constituent agencies.

In fact many strategic forums do have seconded staff, usually a co-ordinator and sometimes a small secretarial support team. It is always worth asking why they have done that. Is it because the partnership doesn't trust its constituents to allow their own staff to take a lead from the partnership as a whole? Is it a statement of commitment to the partnership, to demonstrate that it actually runs something? I'm not suggesting that it is wrong for a forum to do this but it is important to understand why it was done in the first place and what implications it has for going forward.

SUMMARY

This chapter has proposed that there should be a sequence of questions in the life of any partnership.

1. What do its members hope to achieve?

2. What objectives will take them along the road to improvement?

3. How do they plan the changes needed to deliver the objectives?

4. How do they commission and manage the changes they propose?

CHAPTER 4

Who is Involved?

INTRODUCTION

People, of course, are what any collaborative arrangement is about. So obvious a fact is sometimes lost in the swirl of activity surrounding exciting new adventures (or frightening new prospects, depending on your inclinations). People are a complex mixture of self-interest and altruism, curiosity and fear of the new, rationality and emotion, trust and suspicion, love and hate. We seek social and group approval but want to be independent and to make our own decisions. We are a tribal species. Whether this is expressed in crude racial or class terms or in more sophisticated modern guises like professional or political groupings, it is a factor that still needs to be managed.

The contextual factors

Another major factor to bear in mind is that when people are sitting round a partnership table they seldom merely represent themselves. They belong to bureaucracies or groupings which they need to accommodate and which place them under pressures that are not always apparent. Ask yourself the following questions:

- Do they have a 'professional' agenda?
- Who is watching them; what kind of organisation do they represent?
- What power do they have to decide and what must they refer to others?
- What timescales do they operate to?
- Is their financial agenda constrained by profit and loss, budget or procedure?
- What external factors influence the subject under discussion?

(Fletcher 1998)

Partnership planning that ignores these competing drives and external imperatives will simply fail. There are many people with a stake in what happens in the partnership, not all of whom are necessarily represented. They are the 'stakeholders'. Those not directly represented are discussed in the section 'How and where to consult' later in this chapter. The point here is that the representatives must be able to accommodate the interests of those they represent. If they are not enabled to do that, they will stop you in your tracks if they can and slow you down to a crawl if they can't. The partnership facilitator or driver needs to develop the skills of inclusion and negotiation to a high level.

In this chapter we consider some of the more important issues shown in Figure 4.1.

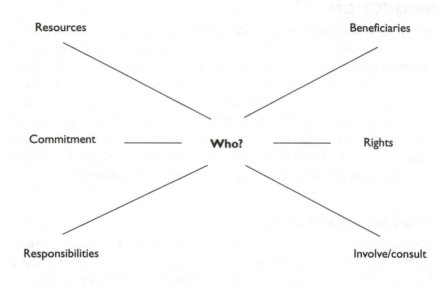

Figure 4.1 The 'stakeholder' issues

BENEFICIARIES

The primary beneficiaries of a partnership are, or should be, the service users, actual and potential. If it can't be shown to benefit them at some point in its development, it is not justified. This rather trite statement of the obvious takes no account of another important consideration. All the other stakeholders must be beneficiaries as well.

For a committed professional the benefit may be the satisfaction of being able to do a better job without other reward. But she will almost always face some costs associated with change. They may simply be the commitment of time and effort to making a new arrangement work. But change may have more serious professional consequences. Closer working may seem to imply the surrender of hard won professional territory. A new approach may have job consequences implying relocation, loss of status or, worst of all, redundancy. Turkeys don't vote for Christmas!

For politicians, too, there are consequences which may not be entirely attractive. Any concerned politician will want to see services improve as a result of action taken on her watch. But the gains are likely to be subtle and long-term for the most part. There will be few votes at stake – though of course there may be many in consequence of a disaster that results from a failure to take action. Politicians also like to control things, on the whole. Any partnership, even at the level of a collaboration in the sense discussed earlier, has the consequence of a certain loss of sovereignty among its members. Once you agree to take account of the views of others in the process of reaching decisions, you forgo a degree of unilateral action. Setting up a management partnership implies much greater pooling of sovereignty. Think of the political debate about the extent of our loss of control in the UK as a result of membership of the European Community, for example. It is always a cost to balance against the benefit.

For every development that is contemplated all the partners need to consider the following questions:

- What is in this for all the clients of my service, including those outside the remit of this partnership?
- What is in this for me?
- What is in this for my constituents, those I represent, back in the agency (and perhaps beyond)?
- What price do we all have to pay?
- What is the benefit and cost for all the other partners, their clients and their users?

An honest effort to identify and share information about these pressures and demands is an important first step towards finding ways of addressing them.

RIGHTS

There is not a great deal about rights in recent literature on partnerships in social care and the whole issue of individual rights seems in retreat just at present in western societies. Perhaps the impact of 9/11 has altered our perceptions of safety. There may be a feeling that, if rights might get in the way of security, they should be forgone.

But the 'crackdown' on crime and anti-social behaviour has been gathering pace in the United Kingdom for much longer, over at least the past 15 years. There are theories about what caused the shift from relative tolerance to the current illiberal climate. The most interesting of them, to my mind, links the shift in public perception of danger which has taken place following the ending of the Cold War and the loss of a clearly identifiable external enemy. Whatever the reasons, the fact that this shift has taken place is hard to dispute.

Public attitudes are contradictory in some ways. While there seems currently to be a clear majority in favour of 'crackdown' to control 'the enemy within', at some cost to civil liberty, there is increasing distrust of the agents of government (who are presumably responsible for enforcement) and of government itself.

The first point to make in this context is that the partnership cannot start from the assumption that the public, and especially the target population, regards it as necessarily benevolent. That perception needs to be earned.

The second point is that the target populations of the relevant partnerships are often themselves 'the enemy within'. It is not the rich, powerful and successful whose rights are at risk but the vulnerable, the noisily disruptive, the 'beggars and winos' (Jack Straw, former Home Secretary, cited in *The Observer*, Sunday 8 October 2000), the 'thugs and vandals' (David Blunkett, former Home Secretary, cited in *The Guardian*, Tuesday 24 June 2003).

This is not to suggest that it is the rôle of these partnerships to challenge government policy, though it may be appropriate to demonstrate the consequences of it on occasion. But it is important for them to be aware of the impact of such policies on their target group and for members to seek to reach a common understanding of them.

The third point to consider is the impact of partnerships themselves on individual rights. There is no doubt that the primary motivation for forming a partnership is that it will deliver a better, more rounded service to the user. But, in the words of one of George Bernard Shaw's characters, 'All professions are conspiracies against the laity.' When they come together the potential for a really effective conspiracy is greatly increased! The best protection against this possibility is close involvement of users and carers.

An issue of particular sensitivity is *information sharing and confidentiality*. In the spirit of co-operation and more effective targeting of services there is often pressure to consolidate information systems and data. This is usually a positive development but at every turn it needs to be examined.

- What benefit will flow from this development?
- What invasion of personal liberty does it entail?
- Is it possible to achieve the benefit without the invasion?

- How do we inform and involve users?

- Is confidential information compromised?

- Are the consequences of not sharing information greater than those of doing so?

A clear example of the conflict between rights and security which is central to many social care partnerships is demonstrated by the recent history of child protection. For the entirely legitimate purpose of the paramount need to protect children, the normal protection of family privacy may be overridden. That the rights of the parents have been set aside in the interests of a higher cause should not be allowed to obscure the fact that they have indeed been set aside.

Even in such a clear arena as child protection, vigilance is required to ensure that we are acting on the basis of reasonable evidence. A recent (2004) report by the Welsh local government ombudsman on a case in Pembrokeshire which had been reported to him showed that the mere suspicion of child protection, with little or no evidence, had been enough for the authorities to act in an extremely high-handed and intrusive way, overriding the normal rights of the family without thought to the consequences if their thinly evidenced suspicions turned out to be wrong.

INVOLVEMENT AND CONSULTATION

One of the best means of ensuring that rights are protected is by involving those whose rights might be infringed in developing the services for which the partnership has accepted responsibility. It is also an essential contributor to:

- agreeing the mission and purpose of the partnership

- identifying objectives and priorities

- testing outcomes.

Some discussions on *consultation, participation* and *involvement* make nice distinctions about the meaning of these three words. I have not been greatly concerned with these distinctions in what follows.

- The *involvement* of stakeholders, especially service users, is what we are trying to achieve.

- Their *participation* is what happens if we do achieve it.

- *Consultation* is the means by which we seek it.

They are, in other words, aspects of the same purpose and process.

The issues governing consultation and involvement are shown in brief in Figure 4.2.

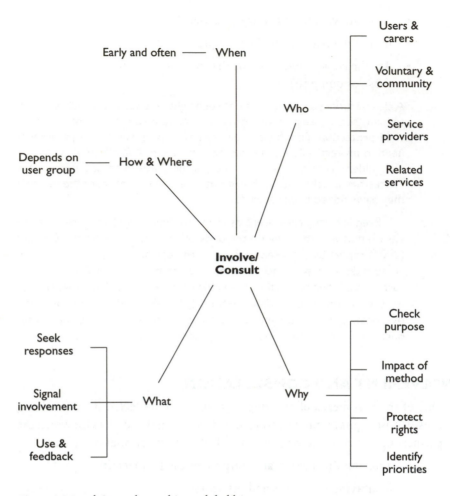

Figure 4.2 Involving and consulting stakeholders

Why consult?

The mission and purpose of the partnership has to be more or less in line with what users and carers want and other interests expect. It is unlikely that they will have been developed in consultation with the full range of stakeholders. So it is particularly important to consult the people who have not been directly involved in their development.

Further down the line specific solutions will begin to take shape. They will represent change for users and others in the way the services affected are experienced. These changes need explaining as clearly and simply as possible. Are they likely to improve access to better services? Are there downsides which have not occurred to partnership members?

Shared information is an inevitable outcome of effective partnership. Users and others affected by this exchange need to understand that it is taking place and the reasons for it. From their perspective the fact that everybody appears to know their business can be very threatening. At least when the services were fragmented and separate you could be fairly sure that they didn't know your business until you told them. There may have been many doors to knock on and multiple forms to complete and questions to answer. But it did provide a sort of backhanded protection which prevented nosy professionals knowing more than they needed! We are all now the target of a thousand databases. If you feel disempowered to begin with, you need to understand why all the professionals know all about you without asking you, otherwise the sense of disempowerment and 'objectification' is further increased.

Consult for what?

When you consult others outside the partnership you need to be clear what you intend to do with the responses they make and what the purpose of the consultation is. You need to:

- signal the kind of involvement you expect from them
- seek the sort of responses you want
- make use of the information you receive
- feed back the uses you have put it to and the changes (if any) which have followed.

There has been some tendency to consult so that the 'consult' box can be ticked. Several government departments in the past sent out consultation documents (and perhaps occasionally still do) with impossibly short deadlines. As they are going to large bureaucracies like local authorities and membership organisations with slow turnround times, short deadlines render unachievable the internal consultation which is necessary to produce a rounded response.

> Local agencies sometimes do 'consultation as process' too. I have been consulted quite recently, as a member of my local community, in an exercise on the options for tertiary health care for the area. I received a glossy brochure on the options for siting a new general hospital. In effect the brochure said, 'These were the three options available from which we chose Option A. You are invited to agree with us.' It was, in other words, dressed up as consultation but the key decision had already been made.

It is excellent practice to inform people about what you are doing but it is not consultation and if it is dressed up as that it tends to provoke frustration rather than involvement.

Who to consult

You should not assume that all the partners within the partnership are equal. Because a person or an organisation is a member of the partnership does not necessarily mean that their view has been taken into account. Decisions negotiated in detail between key players in the strategic health authority, the relevant NHS trust and the local authority social services department are sometimes brought to a strategic forum for the rubber stamp of approval. Consultation within the partnership needs to be robust, as well as that with those outside it.

There are four broad groups to consider:

- service users and carers and potential users
- service providers
- providers and commissioners of related services
- political, voluntary and community interests.

We need to consider how to consult each group in the most effective way (see 'How and where to consult' below), and what they are likely to be interested in. But there are some dangers involved in second-guessing what other people are interested in. It was sometimes assumed, for example, that service users would only really be interested in how the service would affect them personally and would be indifferent to broader strategic and resource management issues. No doubt that is true for some people, but thoughtful service users have insights into the way services interact with each other and fit or don't fit into the whole pattern of their lives, which professionals will never acquire without involving them.

Many service users and carers want to be actively involved. Look at the list of activists in most charities. Many of them, or family members or friends, are suffering or have suffered the hardship which is at the centre of the charity's concern. They want to make things better not just for themselves but for others in a similar position.

A partnership should not be an exclusive business. The groups directly involved in it are of necessity going to be limited but there are many other stakeholders. They will have interests in different aspects of the partnership's business. Where they do have an interest, their perspective may be of critical importance and they do need to be consulted.

When to consult

There is a tendency, especially when there has been a hard won breakthrough of understanding where none previously existed, to want to develop things 'on our own until we are clear/reach agreement. Then we can put it out to consultation.' It is certainly helpful to be in a safe environment where we can throw ideas round without feeling at risk, and watch them disappear without a sense of loss as their weaknesses are exposed in discussion.

But that very reasonable desire needs to be kept in check. There is a fine line between the kind of group thinking in small safe teams which can be so productive, and the 'Them and us', 'They simply don't understand the issues', 'We don't want to say anything to raise expectations' lines which are sometimes the next step along the exclusive road.

The general dictum on consultation is that the more fully you can involve stakeholders in *developing* ideas, the more you can take account of their ideas and the more they themselves will own and invest in the result. So consult early; consult often. The balance to be struck, however, is to achieve this without reaching 'consultation atrophy'. Nothing ever gets done without everyone in the world being consulted and all being in agreement. Under those conditions nothing ever does get done.

How and where to consult

It is important to remember to involve and consult all the stakeholders, not only the service users. Even in a broad partnership there will be many key players who are represented at some distance by those round the table. And there will be even more who are not represented at all. The more all-embracing the partnership becomes in terms of its membership, the more unworkable it becomes (and incidentally the more tokenistic its meetings become). The answer to this in general terms is not to widen the membership more than is necessary to pursue the purpose, but to set up efficient processes of consultation and involvement of people outside the immediate circle.

The method of consultation has to be specific to the people consulted. Formal meetings are obviously inappropriate ways of finding out the views of young children, but a well designed questionnaire which is administered and facilitated by a skilled enabler (such as a teacher) may be a very good method. During the past ten years or so there has been a growing body of painfully learned good practice in consulting individuals and groups whose opinion has been marginalised for social, status, educational or intellectual reasons. The key principles are that:

- the setting must be comfortable
- the issues must be accessible and relevant to the group
- the purpose of the consultation must be clear

- there must be feedback on the impact of the consultation on the outcome.

But how these principles are achieved will vary with the needs of the specific group. Some local authorities, voluntary bodies and housing associations have developed sophisticated methods of communication, but there is not a great deal of material summarising this learning and so it has to be hunted out using information networks. Perhaps the best single source of user involvement information for different groups is the Joseph Rowntree Foundation series *Findings* (www.jrf.org.uk). *Effective Practice in Health and Social Care: A Partnership Approach* (Carnwell and Buchanan 2005) also contains a number of user-specific illustrations of engagement and consultation.

RESPONSIBILITIES

This was formerly one of the biggest rocks on which partnerships foundered. Irrespective of their individual commitment to the purposes for which the partnership had been formed, the first responsibility of all those round the table was to their own line of accountability. Each of the agencies wanted their own business attended to first. The joint agenda was seldom a key priority. To put the problem in current parlance, 'The significant drivers were not at the table'. With government policy now committed to whole systems services, that has changed.

There is still a heavy agency commitment to government targets outside the partnership. No health trust can afford to take its eye off the waiting-list ball as a short-term priority, for example. But social services, health and, more recently, education are increasingly judged on their practical commitment to the development of seamless services which entail active collaboration with other agencies. It is now a key objective of all agencies. Political and management leadership are now increasingly likely to be in the driving seat of the partnership rather than undermining it. At least in principle there is less conflict of responsibility between the members of the partnership as individual agencies and the partnership as a whole than there has ever been.

> Until recently I was a member of a Department of Health sponsored 'performance action team' working with social services authorities in difficulty (the so-called 'zero star authorities'), almost continuously for about two years. I worked in four places in rapid succession and knew quite a lot about some of the other authorities in the same situation.
>
> Apart from the difficulties they experienced in demonstrating and usually delivering a good service, they did not have a great deal in common. Some, for example, were poorly resourced by comparison with their cohort of authorities, but some were not. Some experienced very close political

scrutiny; some did not appear to be part of a political bureaucracy at all. But the one characteristic they all had in common was that each of the departments, and for the most part each of the divisions within the authorities, worked in substantial isolation from each other. Their relationships across boundaries were at best distant and at worst actively hostile. In the jargon of the setting they 'worked in silos'.

This was not of course lost on the Department of Health. It was an active demonstration of the impact of their policy (at least as a negative). 'If you don't work effectively together, poor services are the result (so we will look to see that you do).'

But 'the partnership as a whole' continues to present a problem for the majority of social care partnerships that are not legal entities. There is no clear accountability for what they do, only for those parts for which individual partners have statutory responsibility. This is changing, with, for example, the development of children's trusts; but it is a real problem where a legal entity does not exist: the partnership as a whole cannot accept responsibility as a whole.

RESOURCES

In spite of the strong 'in principle' reasons to develop active collaboration it is not always easy to get the constituents to sign up to resourcing joint effort. This can be for several reasons.

- In order to commit serious money to an integrated activity it has to be explicitly identified as of higher priority than some unilateral expenditure which it will replace – always a big step.

- It's one thing to develop open, honest and mutually respectful dialogue. It is a much bigger thing to cede a degree of control over resources for which you are publicly accountable.

- Staffing issues such as salaries and terms and conditions of service can be something of a nightmare aspect of an integrated service. However keen staff are to work collaboratively with professional colleagues, people working at the same professional level soon become agitated about differences in service conditions.

- However hard the planners have worked at strategic integration, there is always a myriad of practical administrative problems nobody thought of until operational planning begins in earnest. Sorting these things out is an additional cost for which, usually, there has been no budget allocated. If the cost is too great the whole project may begin to be seen as too difficult.

In short, there must be compelling reasons, in terms of improving the quality and effectiveness of service delivery, for going down the route of *integration* (as opposed to collaboration). It depends where the partners are starting from and what the gains might be, but it is safe to say that a leap from 'silo working' to complete integration is almost certain to burst the newly grown bonds of trust, however desirable the result might be in principle.

COMMITMENT

As we said at the beginning of the chapter, people and their attitudes are at the heart of any partnership. If they are committed to making it work, almost all other hurdles are surmountable; if they are not, small obstacles are too great to overcome. Commitment needs to be worked at.

- Is everybody signed up to the purpose of the partnership?
- Is there a set of shared values?
- Is there an agreed standard of behaviour?
- Is there a shared commitment to quality?
- Do we speak the same language?
- Do we have ways of resolving conflict?

The 'Barnsley mouse mat'

Barnsley Metropolitan Borough was one of the very early players in the now widespread concept of strategic partnership. The Local Authority and the NHS established Barnsley Partnership in Action during 1998/99 and it is now a mature development with an interesting history. You can find out more about it by visiting the relevant page of the Integrated Care Network website (www.integratedcarenetwork.gov.uk/resource_view.php?resid=165).

In the early stages the partners agreed a code of conduct which they called 'Rules of Behaviour'. They printed on a mouse mat the summary which I have reproduced below, and made it widely available within the borough.

Purpose

To ensure that all meetings and processes within Partnership in Action are conducted according to the following values and ways of behaving.

Values

Openness and honesty – it is a shared responsibility to ensure that all are able to express opinions in safety.

Participation and equality – anyone's contribution is to be recognised and valued.

Open to challenge – all within Partnership in Action may be challenged in order that we should learn and change.

Fairness – all must ensure that everyone involved has an equal voice by whatever means are appropriate.

Accountability – everyone is ultimately responsible to the people of Barnsley through the framework of accountabilities explicit in Partnership in Action.

Behaviour

Respect and accept other people's contributions, even if you disagree.

Listen, you may learn something.

Be patient, recognise and accept differences in people's ability to communicate.

Use clear, simple English.

Make sure that everyone has the support they need in order to contribute fully.

Explain processes clearly.

Recognise and record minority views.

Quality

The processes and meetings conducted within the Partnership in Action framework will be routinely measured against the values and behaviours set out above. Responsibility to ensure they are adhered to lies with us all.

The 'Barnsley mouse mat' expresses almost everything which needs to be said about gaining the personal commitment of participants in the partnership process – except that engagement in the process itself develops a sense of teamwork and mutual trust. Even the process of addressing and resolving conflict can serve to strengthen the solidarity of the group.

SUMMARY

In this chapter we have considered some of the more important aspects of partnerships as agreements between people. We have concentrated on the logic of working across boundaries with others who may have different imperatives. We have considered their rights and responsibilities and how to communicate with them.

We have not considered the emotional aspects of behaviour to any extent. People have likes and dislikes, hopes and fears; they are aggressive, defensive, generous or mean by individual disposition and under different circumstances. We haven't considered these emotions and their consequences because they extend well beyond partnership and into every interaction. You will find a fuller treatment of these issues in my book *Negotiation for Health and Social Service Professionals* (Fletcher 1998).

Finally, Figure 4.3, drawn from an evaluation of the Mini Sure Start programmes by Partnership at Work and Associates and originally described by Benson (1975), succinctly encapsulates the people aspects of partnership.

Achieving ideological consensus *'What common goals do we have?'*	Building mutual respect and positive evaluation *'How do we feel about one another?'*
Agreeing domain consensus *'What part does each of us play?'*	Achieving work co-ordination at the 'point of practice' *'Who does what, today?'*

Figure 4.3 The people aspects of partnership

CHAPTER 5

Geography and Demography

INTRODUCTION

This chapter is about a collection of not very closely related issues of geography and demography which impinge on the management of partnerships in various ways. It is about:

- boundaries

- communities

- equity.

I have confined myself entirely to those aspects of geography and demography which impinge directly on partnerships; so it is not about issues such as rurality, urban density, travelling times, peripatetic services and so on, important though those things are to the delivery and design of services. Different partners may be accountable for different geographical areas and will be accountable for and to different groups of people. This chapter is about identifying the conflicts which might arise from that and planning to address them. The ground covered here is shown in Figure 5.1.

BOUNDARIES

Many years ago I was an assistant area children's officer working for the old Lancashire County Council, a huge local authority at that time with a population of about 2.5 million. Part of my job was to represent my area of the children's department on the planning team (I use the description very loosely!) for Skelmersdale new town. Another assistant area children's officer was there to represent the other area which covered part of the new town. The health service had three divisions but they were not usually represented. The education service had two (but they were different from ours), as did the welfare department and the public health (including mental health) service, all of which were separate within the county council at the time. Most of the civil service functions like social security were divided along regional lines, as were the utilities. The trouble with that was that the new town area lay smack between Merseyside and SELNEC (a long defunct regional grouping; it was an acronym for South East Lancashire and North East Cheshire).

I'm sure you can imagine how much co-ordination of effort was actually achieved.

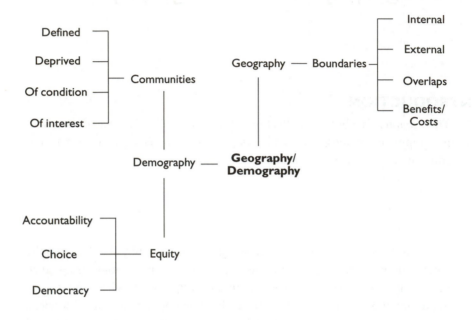

Figure 5.1 Aspects of geography and demography

Fortunately things are no longer quite as randomly confusing as they were in that case. Quite frequently now there are no physical boundary problems at all. Unitary local authorities usually have the same boundaries as NHS primary care trusts (PCTs) in England or local health boards in Wales, for example. Even within the larger authorities where there is more than one PCT they fall wholly within one local authority boundary. Internally most authorities now co-ordinate their divisional boundaries so that the departments are co-terminous.

Even so, there are still difficulties. Specialist NHS trusts in England, for example, sometimes overlap community trusts rather untidily and cover more than one local authority area. Cross-boundary co-operation to provide a joint service across two or more authorities always encounters boundary problems of equity, cost and control.

Imagine, for example, a joint mental health service provided by a specialist NHS trust covering two local authority areas. They have negotiated to provide an integrated, jointly managed service. It can be done, and sometimes has been (see Appendix I for an example in practice). But the boundary issues are a major consideration. Staff from the different services, often doing very similar things within the integrated 'seamless' service, have different conditions, rates of pay, pensions and holiday structures. Accountability for one part of each geographical half of the service is through the individual local authorities. For the 'health' part it is unitary for the whole area. The head of the service has to report to a structure which takes account of the fact that the different components of the services have different funding streams, statutory justification and political accountability.

Now imagine that both authorities have decided to integrate into a single service: all the cross-references and issues to be reconciled would be squared rather than doubled. There is a limit, however ill-defined, beyond which practical considerations outweigh service-level advantages of integration.

Geographical boundaries are not a problem for effective collaboration but they are for any level of integration. Even joint planning becomes very difficult if you are talking about the populations of different localities.

COMMUNITIES

Communities sometimes identify themselves and are sometimes formally identified. Either way, the boundaries they put round themselves, or have put round them, don't necessarily fit comfortably with bureaucratic concepts of partnership for service providers.

Hypothecated finance is often targeted at economically deprived communities and regions. On the large canvas, European Union Objective One funding for the latest phase has been directed towards the most deprived regions in the United Kingdom. On a much more detailed canvas the Sure Start programme of child development for younger children has been targeted at socially and economically deprived communities.

At local level, local authorities try to focus this kind of finance where they conceive it to be most needed – but it isn't always obvious where that should be. Certainly disadvantage does cluster. The indices of multiple deprivation – multiple occupancy, unemployment, single parenthood, low income, poor housing, lack of amenities – tend to gather and to have a multiple impact: poor health, mental illness, low educational attainment, petty crime and disorder, child abuse and domestic violence.

But whereas the key funding stakeholders can probably agree about these community indicators, they are almost certain to have other targets bearing down on them to meet the needs of the wider, less vulnerable communities. In the longer term addressing the impact of deprivation will probably help address these other targets, but political pressures are very often short-term!

Almost all hypothecated finance is time-limited. It will be the local agencies who pick up the eventual financial responsibility when the targeted cash flow ceases. Second, the hypothecated finance is seldom sufficient alone to reverse the problem. It needs additional support from local sources if it is to have the desired impact. Finally, it is not unknown for local agencies to use hypothecated finance to relieve the burden on locally funded services – in effect to shift resources to other targets of their own preference. It is remarkably difficult to spot that this is happening if it is done with any subtlety.

The preceding two paragraphs represent a worst case scenario. In spite of these possibilities, the evaluations of the two examples I gave, Sure Start and Objective One funding, both appear to show a significant impact. But it is important for partnerships to be aware of the potential for these factors to arise in order to reach agreement about how to prevent them.

A further significant issue is that communities, and of course individual families, don't follow neat demographic boundaries. Rich enclaves exist in poor areas, completely distorting the data. Poor, demographically invisible enclaves are sometimes hidden in rich areas. More sophisticated analysis, based increasingly on postcodes rather than registration sub-districts, helps to improve identification, but it doesn't necessarily solve the problem.

> A small, economically deprived estate in South Wales, sandwiched between two comparatively affluent areas but at some physical distance from both, had no public or voluntarily owned social facilities at all. The people on the estate even had to cast their vote in the front room of one of the houses. A socially active group on the estate was desperate to build a village hall to provide a venue for local facilities and events. But the local authority was not initially sympathetic: 'Not in a deprived area; too small to sustain the hall on its own (not responsible enough to run it).'

> The Millennium Commission had funded a programme for building village halls in Wales about this time but, to qualify, the halls had to be free from local authority control (!) and 50 per cent funded from resources raised from within the community. For a small estate with high unemployment, low wages and no middle class, raising even a few hundred pounds was a major achievement. The condition seemed completely impossible to meet, and incidentally to favour already affluent communities.

The good news for partnerships facing obstacles of this kind is that, in spite of these difficulties, the community managed to get its hall built despite the pressure of an adverse postcode lottery. It illustrates the earlier point that, if the people in the partnership are strongly focused on a shared objective, most obstacles can be overcome.

EQUITY

There are inherent political contradictions in the concept of equity, which simply means 'fairness'. Everyone believes in it, but your political philosophy determines what you think it is. The contradictions are rarely acknowledged politically, but complete equity cannot co-exist with local democracy. If the people vote for a party which wishes to invest more public capital in one area, they are also voting to reduce it in other areas. Next door the emphasis might be quite different.

This is not usually a significant problem within partnerships in the United Kingdom, where to a greater and greater extent social policy is determined by central government in England and the national governments in Northern Ireland, Scotland and Wales. Local government is largely responsible for management but purpose has been determined elsewhere. In other words, the key funding partners are unlikely to disagree about it because they have the same ultimate master. Even since devolution the problem has not arisen, at least to date, because social policy has been fully devolved. What would happen in a situation where Westminster and the national administrations took on a very different political complexion of course remains to be seen.

A partnership is unlikely to encounter problems of equity in its financial and legal accountability upwards, but local interpretation of what equity means may well be different from that of the partnership. It is important to take the local stakeholder community with you, at the very least by being completely explicit about the principles behind decisions as well as about the decisions themselves. If, for example, you decide to focus substantial extra resources on a particular deprived community or on a particularly vulnerable user group, you have, of course, also decided to reduce the overall level of spend on the rest of the benefiting population. Unless you are clear about the principle on which the action is based, some of that population will see that concentration as unfair. Some of the local population may still regard the partnership's decisions as inequitable in spite of understanding the explanations for them. But at least they can exercise their view through the democratic process if they disagree with them.

During the late 1980s and early 1990s there was a general professional consensus supported by key politicians about handling juvenile crime by a broad policy of diverting young offenders away from the criminal justice system. It was systematically monitored and was beginning to show some impact on the level of youth crime, as well as achieving its primary purpose of reducing the damage to the young people themselves.

But not enough attention was paid to explaining the principles to the public and the media, and a growing backlash against 'feather-bedding young thugs' eventually caused the loss of political support. The media found a number of multiple offenders as a focus for public hostility and the policy was finally sunk without trace as a result of a horrific high profile murder case (James Bulger, aged 2 years, in 1993). The case itself had nothing to do with the policy, but that of course did not matter. The real damage had been done much earlier by the failure to illustrate the equity benefits to victims of crime as well as to offenders.

SUMMARY

In this chapter we have discussed the complications which arise:

- when partner members are responsible for serving different populations
- when partner members have to balance the priorities of whole communities against targeted vulnerable groups
- when public perceptions of equity diverge from those of the key members of the partnership.

The chapter has identified the issues to be addressed in planning – but there are few generalised solutions.

PART THREE

Partnership in Practice

CHAPTER 6

Managing Change

INTRODUCTION

This chapter and the next one are about how to turn a general strategy, a series of broad objectives, into a new kind of service which will reflect and develop the intention. For the sake of clear illustration I am assuming a start from a local strategic forum which has formulated its vision, its mission and its key objectives. This kind of top-down start is, of course, just one of many possibilities, and many people who read this book will be hoping for some insights in how to manage change beginning from service user level or an intermediate stage. The example below is of a quite different starting point.

> An enterprising manager of a residential home for elderly people succeeds in gathering a group of GPs, social workers, physiotherapists, residents and home staff together to consider how they can work more effectively to improve services for residents. The initiative not only succeeds in its primary aim but it causes the participants to consider how the learning might be extended to services for other vulnerable people in the surrounding community.
>
> Before long it becomes clear that, to make further progress, the group must find ways to influence the behaviour of the bureaucracies within which many of them work, but how to do this? They know that the authority area in which they work has established a supra-agency body called the Strategic Forum for Elderly People. They have little idea what this body does, except that it has some responsibility for co-ordinating policy across all agencies. Clearly they must get on the agenda of this body and start to influence the way it functions. They decide on the changes they want to see, then set up a project to work out how best to manage those changes.

The example illustrates that many of the key factors influencing the management of change (which are discussed in this chapter) are generic, whether the change is driven from the top or starts lower down the hierarchy. (Incidentally, in reality it is almost never 'bottom up' from the beginning, in the sense of starting from the initiative of users or carers. A great deal of effort is needed to enable them to play their full part in the process.)

Once a change is initiated, its influence should be felt up and down the hierarchy. It is just as much a process of users influencing staff, staff influencing managers, managers influencing directors, directors influencing politicians, as the reverse of that. A robust partnership has to base itself on a recognition that it is essential for this to happen. It must also bear in mind that it is harder to be heard from below than from above. Much greater effort needs to be devoted to facilitating communication from below and allowing the voices of users and carers and front-line staff to be heard.

The ground we will cover in the next two chapters is illustrated in Figure 6.1. In this chapter I discuss background, organisation, process and consultation.

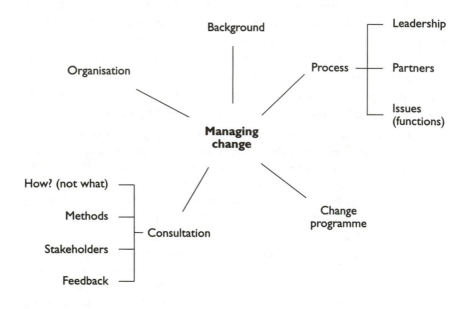

Figure 6.1 Managing change

BACKGROUND

The background of the partnership is of critical importance. I discussed it fairly extensively in the introduction to this book and there is no purpose in simply repeating it here. But it is worth reminding ourselves that the background factors which govern what is strategically possible also have a heavy influence on what is operationally and organisationally possible. There is little chance, for example, that you will be able to move in one step from a recent history of mutual suspicion and distrust between agencies to a fully integrated service.

ORGANISATION

'Form follows function' is a cliché – but one which should be pasted above every 'new broom' chief executive's desk. Structural change is not a necessary precursor to effective improvement of function, so one organisational option available to a partnership is to leave accountability, political control and funding largely as they are, changing only those things which evidently present obstacles to the desired direction of change.

Options

The Children Act 2004 prescribes that every relevant local authority in England (but not in Wales) must have in place a children's trust and a children's director by a date to be specified, which the Department for Education and Skills set at April 2006. A number of authorities had already agreed to pilot this in advance of the requirement coming into force and to share what they were learning from its implementation. They became known as the pathfinder authorities. The Department for Education and Skills commissioned a research project run jointly by the University of East Anglia in association with the National Children's Bureau to discover how the pathfinder authorities were getting on.

In their interim report the team classified the kinds of organisational models the pathfinders had established under four headings. I have not followed their descriptions word for word, but essentially they are as follows:

- integrate pathways and networks
- integrate and co-locate services
- virtual change agent
- joint commissioning.

Detailed variations and combinations of these four models are possible almost without limit, but they seem to me to express the possible broad scenarios pretty comprehensively. Brief synopses of the descriptions in the report are as follows.

Integrate pathways and networks

The organisations are left structurally independent but energy is invested in improving the integration of front-line services by developing, for example, a single assessment process and an integrated database. Collaborative networks of professionals form around user need, as revealed by the assessment, and reform as the need changes.

Integrate and co-locate services

The various professionals are brought together in a single management unit and often in the same physical location. This is a tried and tested arrangement for the management of CAMHS and adult mental health services. There are technical, human resource, and accountability issues; problems to be managed. But experience shows that can be done.

Virtual change agent

This is about the strategic partnership acting as a pressure point for change among its parent agencies. It doesn't necessarily imply structural change but a change in culture and ways of thinking about working together and with users and carers. I would go so far as to say that if this is not happening alongside other changes, nothing much else will change either.

Joint commissioning

Joint commissioning is a single approach to analysis of need, resources, finance and re-engineering across the statutory (commissioning) agencies. To do it across the full range of users who are the target group of a strategic forum, for the first time, is a task of mind-blowing complexity. I speak from experience! A different approach may be to do this first for a specific sub-group, say a special needs group, and use the experience to extend the process in future years.

A mixed approach

In reality, bearing in mind that form should follow function, a strategic forum might be well advised to adopt versions of all these models and apply them to different tasks. There seems to be a growing consensus (see, for example, Thistlethwaite 2004) that a full joint management approach works best for user groups with multiple, complex and closely interacting needs; people with severe disabilities of various types, for example. On the other hand, large-scale but relatively straightforward services, such as community services for vulnerable elderly people in their own homes, may respond best to the integration of pathways and networks, perhaps with the provision of a small 'one-stop shop' to act as the single entry into all the systems.

PROCESS

Three major issues of process to consider are leadership, the rôles of the partners and the key issues.

Leadership

Without a process for turning ideas into action they remain precisely that, ideas. Somebody has to take, or to be given, responsibility for doing something about them. A useful dictum for anyone trying to generate action is 'You can do anything that nobody has said you can't do'.

It is particularly important for local authority people to remember this because the legal and cultural climate appears to say exactly the opposite. The doctrine of *ultra vires* (meaning 'beyond the powers') implies that unless the law explicitly endorses a course of action, you can't do it. I'll leave it to those qualified in public law to define exactly what that means, but it seems to me that, for practical purposes, 'You can't do it' means 'You can't spend money on it'. That in itself is a major constraint, of course, but it should never stop somebody taking a lead in finding ways of getting money spent on something, let alone doing something different.

Someone in the partnership, or a part of it, has to take a lead. In the example in the introduction to this chapter it was someone at operational level, concerned to get a better service for her residents. In another case it could be a local authority chief executive nominating and authorising a senior officer to drive forward the agenda of a strategic forum. It can be almost anyone prepared and able to do it. I labour the point deliberately because one of the principal dangers in a partnership is that taking a lead can seem almost contrary to the spirit of the thing; a denial of our essential equality. Most partnerships are not all that equal to begin with, of course, but even those that are will not get very far if no one is willing to go through the door first.

Selecting the lead

Self-selection, as in the example above, is usually an excellent means of doing this. The person is inevitably committed to the key objectives and enthusiastic to turn them into results. But certain conditions are necessary for success:

- Politicians and senior management must be secure and strong enough to support the assumption of leadership and not to regard it as a challenge to their authority.

- Other professionals must trust the person and his professional group not to take over control and place them in a subordinate position.

- Above all, the person who takes on this rôle must either be skilled in people and change management or receive strong supporting advice from others who have these skills.

Within a strategic forum nomination is much more common than self-identification and the nomination, more often than not, comes from outside the partnership itself. Typically there is an agreement among the main decision-makers in the most powerful parent bodies.

When this happens there may be a degree of wariness and unwillingness, especially at first. The nominated lead can be seen as representing her agency and appearing to place the agency itself in a controlling position. One way partnerships have sometimes sought to avoid this is to bring in an independent chairperson, but I suggest some caution with this solution. It can cause more problems than it solves because the person, though independent, is not on any of the 'inside tracks' and can be seen as both powerless and remote.

The leader must have authority not just within the partnership but on its behalf as well, so external support is essential. In practice this almost always means that a senior officer from one of the major funding partners, either the local authority or the primary care trust/local health board (PCT/LHB) team, takes this rôle. If the chief executive of the PCT or LHB and the local authority throw their weight behind the leader it can be anybody and sometimes the chair is initially taken by a high-profile outsider as we have seen. But there is a difference between chairing and facilitating and leading a partnership. In the end the lead almost always comes from an insider, usually someone from within the local authority or the NHS.

The rôles of the partners

Each partner agency comprises:

- an organisation
- a group of (individual) people
- (very variable) amounts of money
- a set of systems.

Some of them will need to change one or more of these components in order to pursue the key objectives the partnership has collectively set itself. All change demands energy, so by definition there is limited capacity to pursue it. To put it another way, pushing too much change all at once is a recipe for chaos. Change management is the process of identifying a workable change programme and breaking it into manageable projects.

Key issues

The questions to ask in relation to each objective are as follows:

1. What needs to change to move the partnership towards this objective?

2. Why are these changes necessary to achieve the objective?

3. How can the change be achieved?

4. What timescale is necessary to produce the agreed deliverable(s) and can we describe it with enough clarity?

5. What resource will be required to make the change?

6. What priority does this change demand?

7. What pressures drive the change forward?

8. What are the major obstacles in its path?

9. How will we judge its success?

From objectives to deliverables

There are many ways to tackle this challenge but, unless there are compelling reasons for doing it differently, I suggest that the leader, perhaps facilitated by a change agent, goes through each of the five or six key objectives with the significant stakeholders, considering the rôles and potential contribution of each partner member, to make sure that all the ground is covered, and addresses the questions in the previous section.

The more participants there are engaged in this initial exercise, the more ownership there will be of the programme and projects it will eventually lead to. And it will be easier to engage the people and the organisations in the sometimes painful processes to come. The partners have already engaged in a demanding and time-consuming workshop/seminar to agree the mission and key objectives, so I don't lightly suggest that a similar event is needed to agree the change management programme – but it is!

It is tempting, and superficially efficient, to run the two events together. But again, in my experience, that is a mistake. The key objectives need to be agreed among the active members of the partnership and then 'sold' to the less involved parts of the partner organisations. In some cases, like the example at the beginning of the chapter, this may be up through the hierarchy to directing and policy levels. In other cases, such as a strategic forum, it may be down through operational management and front-line staff. Quite often promotion will need to go in both directions at once. Indeed, a key task to cover in considering rôles and contribution to each objective is how best to disseminate the means of addressing it.

CONSULTATION

This is consultation about how to tackle the change agenda. The consultation about what it is intended to achieve should already have taken place. A draft programme which has been well managed politically, using informal networks and opinion leaders, should produce few surprises. But you can never be sure. However well the partners are involved in identifying the change programme, there is a wide range of stakeholders to be consulted. I am assuming, by the way, that by this stage the idea that users and carers are full partners in the enterprise is fully embedded.

Methods

It may be obvious, but the method of consultation should match the needs and normal practice of the stakeholder. Most institutional stakeholders have a well developed means of formulating a corporate view. If they haven't, they need to get one in place urgently. And, as I said before, the groundwork should have been done informally. There should be few surprises.

But a more inclusive approach to governance brings on board groups who may not be used to the traditional bureaucratic systems. Not just users and carers but neighbourhood groups, small charities and other unincorporated groups which have shown a relevant interest may need to be included. For many of them the old method of circular with deadline may not be enough. The alternatives, such as questionnaires and telephone follow-up, should be decided on the basis of the questions, 'How can we facilitate the engagement of this group in this process? What is important to them?'

Information and choice

There should be no confusion between information and choice. It's the difference between 'This is what we have decided' and 'These are the options on which we would like your opinion'. Few things provoke greater irritation than the sort of consultation document which is transparently a *fait accompli* merely going through the obligatory motions.

A favourite ploy is the impossibly short timescale. The internal haggling has typically gone well beyond the time originally planned and the programme managers try to catch up on time by truncating the consultation process. Stakeholders are usually complex networks or bureaucracies. They need time to collate the views of their own internal stakeholders. It may not be intentional, but a three-week deadline for responses is actually insulting.

> Another infuriating trick is to appear to offer options while actually proposing only one. I was recently 'consulted' as a member of my community by means of a flashy brochure about a planned hospital development programme. The strategic health partnership had decided to demolish an old but well loved hospital in one part of the borough and to build a new general unit in a different, more central and more accessible location. They had run into a lot of political flak for obvious reasons. The brochure described the options, told us which one had been chosen and invited us to 'choose' it ourselves. To describe it as an inept piece of opinion management would be over-generous!

Stakeholders

It is always worth reflecting on how the different stakeholders might perceive a proposal. If you get it right you can avoid a lot of unnecessary grief! Consider a proposal to change accountability, say for the purpose of producing integrated management of a project. You may have discussed this *ad nauseum* within the partnership, but are you sure that the stakeholders' views have been properly represented? Are you sure that conclusions reached in the partnership have been fed back to the stakeholder by their representative? Are you sure that they will not see this as a crafty device for snatching control of finance, of policy, of power and personnel, from them?

Note that I am not talking about avoiding conflict here. I am talking about spurious conflict created by misconception and poor communication. I suspect that more problems arise from this than from genuinely conflicting objectives.

Feedback

This is a simple point: if a stakeholder gives you a comment, tell them, in whatever way seems most effective, how you intend to respond to it. It may seem too obvious to be worthy of mention, except that it frequently doesn't happen and it is the single biggest killer of active participation. Nobody likes to be ignored or taken for granted. The worst message of all is 'Your opinion is not important to us'. Interestingly, in the commercial sector and increasingly now in the public sector, there is a growing tendency to believe that all that is required to overcome that message is a recorded announcement saying that it *is* important!

SUMMARY

This is a good point to have a brief recap of the development of a programme and then to look forward through the process as a whole. I have taken the strategic forum as the model for this but the scheme applies in principle to any partnership.

Table 6.1 Summary of the partnership process

Stage	Activity	People/format	Outcome
1. Formation	A period of 'churning' while participants decide what they are trying to do, how they fit in and how far they can trust each other.	Early agendas large, unstructured and undirected. Everyone 'has their say'. First go at user and carer participation usually unsatisfactory because nobody quite knows what they want.	Frustration (typically) leads to collapse or a demand for something better.
2. Vision/mission	Key participants agree on a statement describing the purpose of the partnership.	Best means is a seminar or workshop. Sometimes a parallel event with users and carers works best to involve them.	A short statement of general and specific purpose.
3. Key objectives	Mission developed into 5 or 6 major targets for the partnership.	A further seminar – many advantages in a continuation from the vision/ mission stage.	A list of objectives/an agreed consultation process/a timescale.

Stage	Activity	People/format	Outcome
4. Consultation	A period of negotiation to achieve political and directorial support.	Champions in each agency – format variable for local conditions.	Active support and financial backing for the objectives. Refinements and amendments to the objectives.
5. Programme	A change programme identifying deliverables.	A further seminar following consultation. A programme director, or at least a formal leader, is essential at this stage.	A set of major projects and a list of smaller changes identified.
6. Projects	A project set up for each major initiative.	Project board, leader and team and project initiation document (plan) established.	Celebrate the successful outcome of each project, within budget and to time!
7. Review	(Usually annual) examination of the processes and outcomes, starting again at stage 2.	Large seminar involving as many stakeholders as feasible to review stages 2 and 3. Smaller programme group to review stage 5 following consultation.	Review of projects and revision of programme.

In the next chapter we consider stages 5, 6 and 7 in more detail.

CHAPTER 7

The Change Programme

INTRODUCTION

This chapter is about managing the programme. Most of the skills and knowledge required to do this successfully are generic, but the additional competence you need in doing it for a partnership is an understanding of the special issues involved in working across professional, administrative, legal and political boundaries.

This chapter is emphatically not a course on programme management. There are many courses and books on programme and project management and I have included one or two of the latter in the bibliography. But the programme director needs to be competent in these skills, as do the project managers at their own level. This chapter is intended to provide a checklist, an illustration and an introduction to the process.

However well conceived the aims and strategic direction, the success of a partnership is determined at micro level. It's what happens to the user that matters. Indeed, a partnership at local service delivery level can be successful and effective (if not necessarily sustainable) in spite of chaos and incoherence above, but the opposite is definitely not true.

Throughout this chapter I have described a very definite programme management structure. I don't want to imply that I think this is the only structure which works, or that it fits every situation. All I can say with assurance is that this, or something very like it, has worked before and avoids some of the pitfalls I have witnessed elsewhere. The only aspect of it which is a sine qua non of good partnership management is clear accountability and explicit leadership. Whatever the structure, you need to know who is doing what and who is responsible for decisions.

It might be useful to describe a few of the definitions I have used throughout this chapter. They are repeated as they occur but it is helpful to have them together in one place.

- The *partnership* is all the people nominated by their agencies to represent them in the partnership meetings.

- The *programme board* is the team of between five and seven people chosen by the partnership to run and manage the programme on their behalf.

- The *programme director* is the paid or seconded officer whose responsibility it is to implement the programme.

- The *project executive* is the individual appointed by the programme board to run and oversee a project. It is not a term I would have chosen but the position is described thus in PRINCE2 (the UK government standard project management methodology, of which more later in this chapter) and widely understood by its practitioners.

- The *project board* is the group of people representing various key interests in the project to support the project executive.

- The *project manager* is a (usually full-time) post-holder whose task is to implement the project.

- The *project team* is the support team of people with the skills necessary to undertake different components of the project with which they are tasked by the project manager.

To see where we are, let's just revisit the outline table at the end of the last chapter; the key stages we consider in this chapter are reproduced for convenience here.

Stage	Activity	People/format	Outcome
5. Programme	A change programme identifying deliverables.	A further seminar following consultation. A programme director, or at least a formal leader, is essential at this stage.	A set of major projects and a list of smaller changes identified.
6. Projects	A project set up for each major initiative.	Project board, leader and team and project initiation document (plan) established.	Celebrate the successful outcome of each project, within budget and to time!

Stage	Activity	People/format	Outcome
7. Review	(Usually annual) examination of the processes and outcomes, starting again at stage 2.	Large seminar involving as many stakeholders as feasible to review stages 2 and 3. Smaller programme group to review stage 5 following consultation.	Review of projects and revision of programme.

For readers who find navigation easier in a graphic, mindmap form, the first part of this chapter is outlined in Figure 7.1.

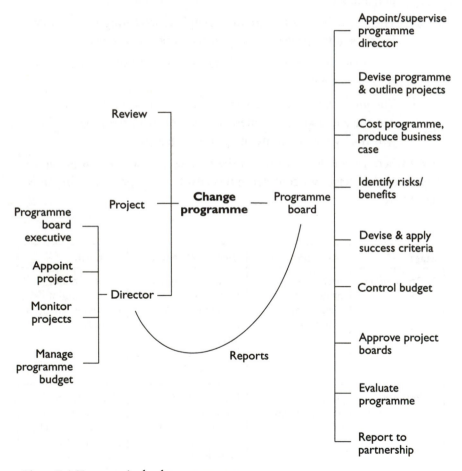

Figure 7.1 Key stages in the change programme

To illustrate the process I have assumed a strategic partnership for services to elderly people. One of the key objectives in their plan to achieve their mission is to strengthen support to elderly people in the community so as to allow them to maintain their independence with a reasonable quality of life. Another is to improve integration between hospital, nursing and residential care so as to reduce trauma, improve transition and avoid bed blocking. Following consultation, the partnership decides to concentrate all its collective energy on designing a change programme to pursue those two key objectives over the next three years.

THE PROGRAMME BOARD

It is clear that a strategic partnership which represents many organisations and typically has over 25 members cannot manage a change programme directly. It must appoint a small *programme board* from among its members. The accountability of the programme board to the partnership as a whole needs to be made completely explicit – and this is often forgotten in practice.

The reason it is so important is that the programme board usually comprises the representatives of the most powerful stakeholders, notably the local authority adult social services and the health authority (certainly in the case of services for elderly people). They control most of the money and want to keep a firm hand on the way the programme is managed. Nothing wrong with that – but it is important that the rest of the partnership does not become marginalised as the pressure begins to build.

The most difficult aspect of partnership working is to strike the right balance between remaining open and inclusive and actually getting anything done. The partnership as a whole cannot, and should not, be involved in second-guessing every decision about running the programme, but it must be assured that the direction of travel does support the agreed objectives and priorities and that the programme is delivering as expected.

> In our example the programme board comprises the assistant director of social services (adult services) and an assistant chief executive from the local authority, two officers of the NHS primary care trust, a consultant geriatrician, the local head of Age Concern (nominated by the voluntary agencies) and the chief executive of a local group of nursing and residential homes (nominated by the care home providers organisation).
>
> The board reports progress to the partnership at its monthly meeting and it must seek approval for the establishment, terms of reference, timeframe and proposed budget for each new project. It is very clear that the board reports to the partnership. Its members do not bypass the partnership and report directly to their parent organisations. Obviously

nobody is going to stop them talking to colleagues 'back at the office', nor should they want to. For example, if the director of social services thought that the board was taking the wrong direction, she might convey that to her board member colleague. But any formal reservation (or proposed withdrawal of support or finance) would be conveyed to the partnership, not directly to the board.

Matters of formal accountability might seem abstruse in the calm period before anything actually happens. But as the action starts, money starts to be spent, slippage starts to occur, egos start to get bruised. A clear and explicit track to follow to resolve difficulties becomes critically important when any of these things happen.

The rôle of the programme board

The principal responsibilities of the programme board are as follows:

- to appoint and supervise the programme director
- to devise the programme and outline the projects
- to cost the programme and submit a business case to the partnership
- to identify and manage risks
- to devise and apply the criteria for success
- to control the budget
- to appoint the board's controller for each project (called, for the remainder of the chapter, 'the project executive')
- to approve membership of the project boards
- to evaluate the programme
- to report progress to the partnership.

Appointing the programme director

This has to be one of the first steps taken by the board. Not much progress is possible without skilled management and leadership and, almost by definition, those board members who may be in a position to provide it will have other major 'day jobs'.

Programme and projects

The board will usually need to start work without the support of the director (who hasn't been appointed yet) on the overall design of the programme. The following is just an illustration of what it might contain but any programme will have longer-term and 'quick win' elements.

- A long-term project aimed at the planned integration of commissioning and service delivery across the whole programme field.

- A 'one-stop shop' aimed at providing a single contact point for all referrals.

- A single assessment system across the programme area.

- A single database accessible, as appropriate, to commissioners and service providers.

- A project designed to integrate services and resources across hospital, nursing and residential care.

- A process evaluation project to look specifically at unnecessary, redundant and clumsy processes across the whole programme area.

By the time the programme director is appointed there will usually be a list of project proposals which comprise the draft programme. His very first task will be to make sure that the list of projects is expressed in terms of the objectives of the partnership, and to gain the board's approval for any redrafting which may be necessary to improve targeting or clarity.

By this stage each project should have a draft *mandate* which describes its purpose and expected result, outline timescale, lifespan, indicative budget and criteria for success. The number, scale and scope of the projects will of course be initially determined by the indicative budget the partnership has allocated to the board (and the funders have allocated to the partnership). At the early stages of programme development nobody will have much more than a 'Think of the number you first thought of' idea of the actual cost of delivering the strategic priorities, and the whole programme should be thought of initially as a working pilot on which a more robust cost/risk/benefit profile can be constructed from experience.

The business case

It may be difficult to construct a full business case before the director is appointed. It is, in any case, a fairly specialised task and one for which a consultant might be a preferred option. The business case is the first systematic attempt to bring together the indicative budget which the board has been allocated, the strategic plan agreed by the partnership and the programme proposed by the board. Inevitably one or more of those three elements will need modification. It would be little short of miraculous for them to match by accident on the basis of initial guesswork. Achieving the reconciliation which leads to a business plan which the partnership can approve will be a major test of good leadership and skilful negotiation.

Risks and benefits

Part of the business case will be an analysis of major risks and benefits. The public sector has tended to be risk averse in the past but, in the social care field in particular, risk aversion is also benefit avoidance! To illustrate this from the field of our example: a preference for residential care for a vulnerable elderly person might seem the safest, in the sense that there is greater risk of falling, for example, in an unsupervised situation at home. On the other hand, once the challenges of daily life are removed, for many people the quality of life deteriorates and the risk of apathy, depression and mental deterioration increases. There are, in other words, no risk-free solutions. A risk analysis is a good way of identifying the best fit to individual needs.

Criteria for success

All the participating agencies will be very familiar with the need to demonstrate both assumptions of positive outcome and the criteria by which they will be measured. They are exactly the same for partnerships. The major challenge is that these assumptions are not necessarily expressed in the same way by the different agencies, nor subject to the same tests of effectiveness. There is a great deal now in print and on the web about performance management, best value, the balanced scorecard and benchmarking. But it is generic or specific to different services rather than to partnerships. It may be possible to use agency-specific criteria for some evaluation; on the other hand it may be necessary to devise new sets for some where the agency criteria don't appear to fit.

Controlling the budget

The director is responsible for managing the budget under the immediate control of the board. The latter must be assured that proper accounting procedures and audit trail are in place and applied. Most of the finance which goes into partnership work is public money; even that which is not is charitable donation. So the normal standards of public sector accounting and reporting apply just as much as they do to the parent partners. The partnership as a whole is ultimately responsible but it must rely heavily on the programme board to exercise control on its behalf.

One of the major difficulties of programme management and account-ability is that, as things currently stand, many partnerships are not incorpo-rated bodies. They don't legally exist. This may change with the creation of children's trusts and more widely for adult services in the future. But for the most part statutory and other incorporated members are responsible for what happens, and only for their own agenda imposed by statute. The issue of accountability, which is expressed in financial terms, is still a grey area. The answer to the question 'Who do I see about that?' is often far from clear. Put another way, where the buck stops is not evident. These are some of the reasons why *de facto* clarity and strong leadership are so critical to partnership success.

Appointing the project executive for each project and approving membership of the project boards

Each of the projects which is established needs its own board chaired by the executive appointed by the programme board. The executive is the programme board's own project controller, so they appoint him. The remainder of the project board (of which more below) are primarily representatives of the major stakeholders, and nominated by them. The programme board will need to limit numbers to a viable management committee – preferably no more than six. And it may be sensible to give the board a specific veto to ensure that the limit is maintained and to avoid unworkable conflicts.

Evaluating the programme

As the partnership's programme management team, the programme board has the primary responsibility for evaluating the effectiveness of the programme as a whole. They will rely on the executive of each project board to report on how she sees its outcomes. They will also have a second strand from the project manager through the programme director. Between the two the board will evaluate the effectiveness of the policy and of its execution.

THE PROGRAMME DIRECTOR

In order for the programme board to deliver a programme it must have resources, of which the most critical is the programme director. Most of the work on the programme will be done in the individual projects which we discuss later but the whole needs to be co-ordinated and directed with the authority of the board.

Whoever he is, the programme director is accountable to the board. He may be a senior officer in any of the participating agencies, seconded full- or part-time. Or the appointment may be specifically for the purpose. It is usual to manage the human resources practicalities through one of the participants. But the director must be a servant of the partnership as a whole and accountable for performance to the board – in effect its chief executive.

Apart from facilitating and executing the responsibilities of the board, the director will have tasks of his own:

- to appoint the project managers
- to monitor the projects
- to monitor the programme as a whole
- to manage the programme budget.

Appointing the project managers

The programme director is responsible for the appointment of the project managers and he must do so in the light of their competence and their acceptability to those on whom the success of the project depends. Such appointments are often negotiated in the context of a complex combination of power and influence, flavoured with a handful of reason and a generous dash of emotion. The programme director needs to be an excellent negotiator!

In the context of appointing project managers, the agencies will be concerned to see someone in that rôle who understands their particular needs and problems (for projects with major significance for their responsibilities). They might prefer one of their own. However that works out, the director must be in a position to satisfy himself that the project managers are competent to do the job.

I can of course write about the need for competent project managers in a planner's guide to my heart's content, but that doesn't make it happen. What *must* happen if the project is to succeed is that the inexperienced project manager should receive some training in project management, and support as needed to carry out the rôle effectively.

Monitoring the projects and the programme as a whole

The board will need to make judgements about the degree to which individual projects are achieving the objectives set for them. The director is responsible for ensuring that the monitoring programmes put in place by the individual projects provide the board with the necessary evidence: it is for each project to set up its own monitoring system, but the director must determine the criteria and judge whether the systems established will meet them.

Once this has been done, he should receive a regular flow of information in a form which enables him to keep an eye on all the projects at once. This implies a limited range of critical indicators rather than a 'haystack in a spreadsheet'. A model now widely used is the 'balanced scorecard'. This presents a limited number of key indicators and highlights only those which are moving against expectation. The analogy often used is the dashboard of a car: it highlights only the information you really need at any time, often in the form of orange or red lights which only appear when you need to pay attention.

The director needs to put the information from all the projects together. In a typical programme some of them at least will be critically inter-dependent. Consider the example of the project list under the heading 'Programme and projects' (pp.89–90). The project to develop a single assessment system and process may be well on target but dependent for its effective implementation on the one-stop shop being up and running. If that project is slipping or facing unforeseen difficulties, it may not be possible to implement the system. The director must consider the options and recommend one to the programme board:

1. develop an interim process

2. speed up the one-stop shop, if necessary at additional cost

3. delay the implementation of the single assessment system

4. some other creative solution.

Managing the programme budget

The board is responsible for identifying and controlling the budget, but it will depend heavily on a robust financial management process to monitor and audit income, expenditure and investment. It is the director's job to put the system in place and make sure that it continues to work properly. She may require specialist help to do it and there will certainly be an external audit as well but, as chief executive, the director is ultimately responsible.

PROJECTS

Up to the point at which the first project is put in place, the partnership has effected little change. Attitudes may be shifting – but they are unlikely to have reached far outside the partnership membership itself, unless there has been a planned approach to doing that. Service users will have noticed little change. The projects are therefore the key means of delivering the vision which the partners have negotiated.

This section is about setting up and delivering a project. There is a great deal of information about project management. Appendices 1 and 2 illustrate specific examples. Appendix 3 is an outline template for project management produced by my own company, SSSP Consultants Ltd, for its clients (2003). The 'gold standard' in project management is *Managing Successful Projects with PRINCE2* (OGC 1998). But you really need to do the course rather than simply read the book to make effective use of it.

In this short framework I have highlighted five key aspects which are particularly important to get right:

- the project executive and the project board
- the project brief
- the methodology
- accountability and reporting
- the project manager.

The process is illustrated schematically in Figure 7.2.

The project executive and the project board

The programme board needs to appoint someone who will report progress on each project and accept ultimate responsibility for delivering it successfully. It must be someone who can be called to account, either by the partnership as a whole or by one of the senior partners. It doesn't need to be someone who is himself a member of the programme board or is even represented on the partnership board. But it must be someone who is not the project manager. In the language of PRINCE2, the UK government standard project management methodology, this is the project executive.

For a small project with a very limited cash budget there may be no need for a project board. For anything larger there will be. Assuming there is a board in addition to the project executive, it should include:

- representatives of the major stakeholders and funders
- a representative of the service provider
- a treasurer or accountant.

The members of the project board have specific rôles. The *stakeholder/funder* representatives are there to protect and represent the interests of the bodies they represent. The *service provider* is there to keep an eye on service interests and to keep the board aware of emerging delivery problems. The *treasurer* is there to exercise financial oversight. It is useful to highlight the difference here between the programme board and the project boards. Members of the

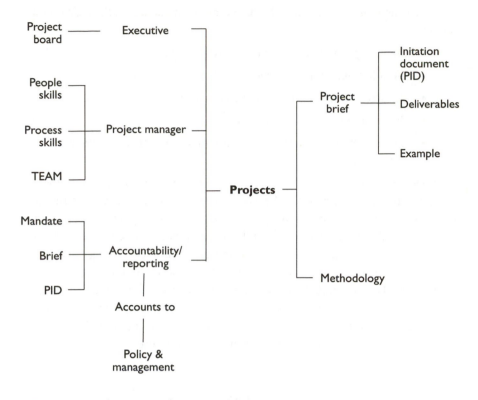

Figure 7.2 Five key aspects of project management

programme board should have different skills and experience but they are all there to act together as the executive board of the partnership. The only thing they represent, collectively, is the partnership. On the project boards only the project executive is there specifically to represent the partnership through the programme board.

The project brief

The project brief is the responsibility of the project executive (supported by the project board if there is one by that stage) but she will develop it in collaboration with the project manager, who will almost certainly draft it. At the time the project executive is appointed there will be a short mandate, perhaps no more than a paragraph, describing the programme board's purposes, intended outcomes and perhaps an indicative budget for the project. The mandate is used as the starting point for the brief.

The brief will be much more detailed than the mandate. At the least it will include:

- the background and information requirements
- intended outcomes by time
- the size and functions of the project team
- the required budget and cashflow
- a Gantt chart or similar device showing key stages and their relationship to each other.

A project brief can be a couple of sides of A4 paper or it can be a full-blown project initiation document (see below), but whichever it is, it should be the product of research and planning in some detail. In Appendix 2, I have included a real project brief, or at least the part of it put out to tender to consultants. Because of its purpose it invites proposals about methodology and cost which would be included in an in-house project. Bear in mind that as partnerships themselves are unlikely to have staffing resources of any size and range, they will be relying on consultancies or ad hoc teams comprising staff from partner organisations anyway. The response from the consultants will form the remainder of the brief. An example of one such response is also included in Appendix 2.

The project initiation document (PID)

The brief is the starting point proper for the project. The first major step for the team is to produce a project initiation document to submit to the executive and the project board. This sets out what each team member will do, by when and with what intended result. Unlike the brief the PID can be amended, with the approval of the project board, to meet new contingencies that emerge. Days allocated to one task can be shifted to another, and a large project should have some unallocated time to meet the unexpected. The unexpected always occurs; it's to be expected!

The deliverables

This is the vogue word for what should come out at the end of the project. If the expected product is a service or process specification, as in the case of the example in Appendix 2, the result of the project should be a report proposing at least the following:

- the *structure* of the proposed service or process; where it will fit; how it will account for its actions
- the *budget* required to start it up and maintain it

- the *staff* required, their *competence, pay* and *conditions*
- the *information* they will require and the system to deliver it
- the *outcomes* to be expected
- the method and benchmarks of *evaluation.*

The methodology

Complex projects require a systematic approach to their management to prevent the bricklayer arriving on site before the bricks. There are several methodologies and frameworks which can be used for this purpose. Some of them are structured to the last detail. Others assume a need to modify the structure in detail to match the project in detail.

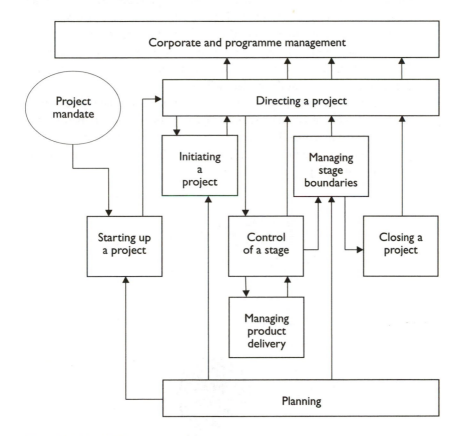

Figure 7.3 PRINCE2 Process model

The gold standard in many ways is the UK government-sponsored PRINCE2 methodology. It is the most exhaustively detailed process I have encountered (see Figure 7.3). It has the dual advantage of being widely used and having a highly prescriptive vocabulary, some of which I have employed in this chapter. The benefit of these two factors is that within the project management 'industry' there is a common understanding of the processes involved in PRINCE2. The official PRINCE2 website (www.ogc.gov.uk/prince2) summ-arises the methodology thus:

> PRINCE2 is a process-based approach for project management providing an easily tailored and scaleable method for the management of all types of projects. Each process is defined with its key inputs and outputs, together with the specific objectives to be achieved and activities to be carried out.
>
> The method describes how a project is divided into manageable stages enabling efficient control of resources and regular progress monitoring throughout the project. The various roles and responsibilities for managing a project are fully described and are adaptable to suit the size and complexity of the project and the skills of the organisation. Project planning using PRINCE2 is product-based, which means the project plans are focused on delivering results and are not simply about planning when the various activities on the project will be done.
>
> A PRINCE2 project is driven by the project's business case, which describes the organisation's justification, commitment and rationale for the deliverables or outcome. The business case is regularly reviewed during the project to ensure the business objectives, which often change during the lifecycle of the project, are still being met.

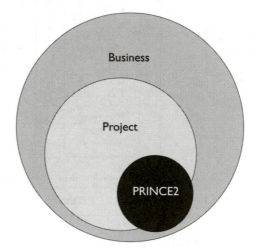

Figure 7.4 Scope of PRINCE2

There are often different groups of people involved in projects: the customer, one or more suppliers, and of course the user. PRINCE2 is designed to provide a common language across all the interested parties involved in a project. Bringing customers and suppliers together typically involves contracts and contract management. Although these aspects are outside the scope of PRINCE2, the method provides the necessary controls and breakpoints to work successfully within a contractual framework.

The disadvantages with employing PRINCE2, and perhaps other highly structured and detailed methodologies, is that they *are* universal. They assume that every part of every process needs to be at least checked off, whatever the type, scope and scale of the project. Second, learning to implement the methodology is no trivial matter. There are several one- and two-day courses in project management on the market which build on existing experience. This is emphatically not one of them!

For an example of the framework approach to project management, see Appendix 3. It was written by me some time ago as a pamphlet in response to requests for something of the sort to help new projects get off the ground with a day or two of facilitative assistance. The framework approach is much less prescriptive than methodologies like PRINCE2 and assumes management skills for using the framework. To some extent the project team has to design the process, but, in doing so, learns something about what will work. The framework assumes that all projects have certain process stages in common.

Accountability and reporting

The line of accountability for a project and how it is delivered is critically important to its control, compatibility with other projects in the programme, other relevant services and ultimately its successful outcome.

Figure 7.5 shows the line of accountability and reporting discussed in this chapter. It's not the only possibility; the absolute requirement is that it is clear and it helps to have it as simple as possible.

Two points in Figure 7.5 should be emphasised.

- The project manager is accountable to the programme director for her performance and competence. She is responsible to the project executive for the implementation of the project.

- The project executive is personably responsible to the programme board to whom he reports. The project board does not have a collective responsibility. Each member of it is accountable to his parent agency/group. The board is there to support the executive and the manager and to safeguard the interests they represent.

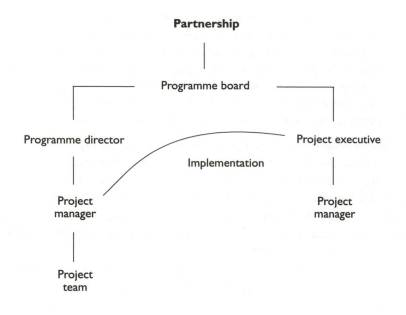

Figure 7.5 The line of accountability and reporting in project management

The project manager

The competence of the project manager is of course critical to the success of the project. The big difficulty facing the programme director in recruiting a suitable post holder, apart from local political pressures, is in finding someone with a suitable work preference profile. A good project manager has two key characteristics.

1.   She is a good people manager, leader and motivator.

2.   She is a highly systematic, almost obsessional, process manager.

It will strike the experienced human resources manager immediately that such a combination of characteristics is very hard to find! People managers, drivers, concluder producers, tend to find the nitty-gritty of process detail rather tedious. People who enjoy following a process through logically and in detail tend to find human vagaries and irrationalities irritating and frustrating. This isn't an issue confined to partnership projects but, given their particular sensitivity and the manoeuvring which characterises them, it is especially sensitive in this context.

The beginning of a solution to the problem is recognition of it, above all by the project executive and the project manager herself. If the project manager is a strong process manager but weaker in other areas, the executive might share the burden of leadership and people management with her. If the project manager is good at leadership and motivation she might be able to look to a member of the project team to take on much of the burden of process management as part of their rôle.

REVIEW

Little needs to be said about reviewing the programme, except that it needs to take place after an agreed period.

- How many projects have been successfully completed and have led to the implementation of the service or proposed outcome?
- What are the next priorities to be included in the programme?
- Are the vision and the mission still an adequate reflection of the aspirations of the partners?
- Are the structural and financial arrangements adequate to support the partnership in developing its future programme?

Above all, the review demonstrates that performance and service management are circular processes rather than linear ones. We plan, we implement, we review, then we plan again. That sentence offers a suitable metaphor for the management of partnership too.

CHAPTER 8

Present and Future

The momentum driving greater 'joined up' governance would not now be easy to reverse. Collaborative working has always been the preferred means adopted by perceptive professionals because they have been able to see the benefit. Its spirit has long been part of the rhetoric of successive governments but they have often acted in ways which discourage it in practice. But that is now much less true. Even when the long predicted financial downturn puts a squeeze on public expenditure, the proposition still makes sense and the culture is becoming stronger all the time.

Wherever we turn, the pressure continues to build to find ways of achieving more effective collaboration. Sometimes the motive is efficiency from reduced duplication and better targeting; sometimes it is better service quality; sometimes it is reduced costs.

There are some continuing big issues which have always been present in any attempt, formal or informal, to establish a partnership approach to providing social care services. There is no reason to assume that they will change in the future. I have referred to them in earlier chapters but they are gathered here all together.

Futurology is a notoriously difficult art. Typically it exposes the speculator's personality, preferences and fears far more than it tells us about the future as it will really be. This closing chapter is not an exercise in gazing into the crystal ball. Experience has taught me that I am not all that good at it. Twenty-five years ago I was a member of a group speculating about what we should do to prepare for the time when oil ran out. It's still a reasonable question, but we never even considered that nature itself would call time by warming up the globe long before that happened.

THE BIG ISSUES

All social care partnerships depend on the presence of a small number of really vital factors. If these are present they will succeed in producing better results, whatever other adverse factors may be present as well. If one of them is weak or absent, chances of success are greatly reduced. They are:

- clarity of purpose
- good leadership
- a positive culture
- commitment to participation
- strong programme management
- sensitive people management.

Clarity of purpose

The partners need to know what they are collaborating for; it needs to be explicitly expressed and the partners and their parent agencies need to engage in the process of agreeing what it is and of finding ways of engaging users and carers in the process. Nothing much else is possible at all without that clear statement of purpose. Without it the 'partnership' continues to be an endless series of meetings to discuss longer and longer agendas.

Good leadership

A paradox of partnership is that to engage the partners fully in the process requires effective leadership and control. There are all sorts of reasons that prevent strong leadership emerging, especially in the early stages when it is most critical of all. No agency wants to be seen to be making a bid for power and control; and no agency wants any other agency to take over and pursue their own agenda to the exclusion of others. Add personalities to the mix, and there are many sensitivities to address. But address them we must eventually, so it may as well be from the outset.

A positive culture

If the key stakeholders in an incipient partnership believe in the idea that working together to find the most effective delivery systems is worth the frustration of doing so, they will act as promoters and supporters. They will challenge the culture of frustration and negativism which is always present at the fringes of change. Problems encountered on the way will be regarded as challenges to overcome, rather than as evidence of impossibility or deterioration.

It sounds almost glib to express the issue in these cheerleader terms. All this 'can do' stuff is mere froth, isn't it? I can point to no research evidence to support the assertion, but my experience strongly suggests that it is critical. If the key players talk informally among their peers and subordinates in terms of reining in the aspirations of colleagues in other agencies and defending their own position, those attitudes permeate and limit development. On the other hand, if the informal talk is of seeking solutions to difficulties, thinking creatively and staying calm and positive in the face of frustration, the corporate mood responds to that and difficulties are in fact overcome.

Commitment to participation

This is not the place to explore the subject of diversity in any detail, but anyone who has examined their motives honestly will recognise their own tendency to seek exclusiveness. Exclusive restaurants, exclusive clubs, exclusive addresses imply a desire to restrict access to those who are rich, or smart, or educated or elite in some other way. A commitment to promoting diversity is the polar opposite and is the foundation on which real participation of users and carers is built.

There are few generalisations possible about how participation is to be achieved. The means of including, for example, adolescents, very elderly people, young children and people with learning difficulties in the construction of their own services and the shape of services in general are bound to be very different. A few groups cannot participate directly in any meaningful sense: people with very severe learning difficulties; infants; people with advanced dementia, for example. But the commitment remains the same. 'How can we infer, as far as we can, what would be the best service from their point of view?'

Strong programme management

We explored programme and project management in Chapter 7. It is included here as a key issue as a reminder that, just as effective leadership is critical to creating a focused policy to which the partners commit, strong programme and project management is the key to turning policy into outcome.

Every public sector management consultant with whom I have ever discussed it identifies slippage as an endemic feature of public sector project management. True, for single agencies it becomes even more of an issue in partnerships. Partnership projects are typically complex. They involve many people and many consents; they involve the engagement of several systems to produce a single result. Slippage under those circumstances is not merely a few months' delay. It often results in a different, usually weaker, outcome than that originally envisaged and sometimes no outcome at all. Money is lost; voluntary commitment is lost; momentum is difficult to regain.

The way to overcome the problem is by competent programme and project directorship undertaken by people who will not be bullied into making promises about delivery that they cannot keep.

Sensitive people management

The people issues which are the very essence of effective corporate management in single agencies are even more critical in running effective partnerships.

In at least one respect the importance of working with the grain of stakeholders' motivation is more clearly recognisable in the management of partnerships. The exercise of control and consent cannot be on the basis of 'Just do it because I say so'. The partners may not be equal in the sense of having equal power; they may not even sit round the table by consent but because an external authority has forced them into that position. But, whatever the illusions, they will not do anything substantial and significant other than by consent. A culture of trust has to be developed.

- Significant change has to be negotiated among those to whom it will fall to deliver.

- Teams have to be built among groups of people who may have come from very different corporate backgrounds (and from some with no corporate background at all).

- Positive attitudes to diversity have to be promoted, sometimes starting from very disparate baselines.

- Corporate attitudes to staff vary greatly within public service agencies. The partners will need to align these attitudes increasingly – especially if staff are expected to work together in unitary teams.

Human resource management varies in many ways. At the immediately apparent level, terms and conditions and salaries are often very different. But there are many less obvious differences concerning:

- permissions (to take leave, to work at home, to take executive action at different hierarchical levels)

- participation in policy formation

- control of budgets
- the explicitness of the command structure (who has the right to take different actions)
- recruitment and retention
- staff support and supervision
- need to know and right to comment.

Together, these differences signal the degree to which staff are controlled, trusted and valued. It is a grave mistake for the partners to assume that these things will be roughly the same within all the partner organisations and that they will not be the cause of tension and stress once people begin to work closely together and compare among themselves their relationships with their parent bodies.

THE FUTURE

As I said at the beginning of the chapter, future prediction is a mug's game, and I'm not going to attempt to speculate about what will happen in the way public sector partnership develops. Your guess is as good as mine. The way future policy supports or disables the big issues I referred to above will be critical. All we can do as individuals is to watch developments critically with that in mind; to object if we see dangers; and to manage within the constraints if our objections fail.

There are a few additional factors which will impinge on the future development in some way, though it is hard to predict exactly how they will operate. Four of them occur to me as being especially significant:

- the current progression of policy
- the uncertainties embodied in those policies
- the policy conflicts inherent in democratic government
- complexities in developing a public sector partnership.

Progression

There have been several references throughout the book to the Children Act 2004 because it is already on the statute book and developments in children's services governance are a few paces ahead of adult services, because they were driven forward by the Climbié report. But the same broad model adopted in England by the Department for Education and Skills for children is being adopted by the Department of Health for adults. It may turn out to have quite a different administrative framework, but the strategic collaborative forum and the single lead director are already in place.

The planning process covered in this book is the same in general terms for both groups. Much of the learning about partnerships for children can be read across to help develop services for adults (and vice versa). In many local areas that is happening because both are under the overall governance of a public service strategic form.

A third spending department, that of the Office of the Deputy Prime Minister, is also promoting partnership through local area agreements designed to simplify funding, strengthen local public service agreements (partnerships) and improve neighbourhood renewal. Finally the 'control' departments, notably the Cabinet Office and the Treasury, are promoting collaboration as a tool for efficiency and better targeted spending.

At least in the short to medium term the policy pressure to continue to develop more extensive systems of collaboration across the various functions of the public and voluntary sectors shows no sign of abating. Anyone who thinks they might be able to get on with their own business undisturbed, until it all dies down, would be well advised to rethink!

Uncertainties

Apart from uncertainties about what might transpire as a result of consultation or shifts of policy, there is considerable uncertainty about how the existing proposals will pan out in practice. In England, for example, there is a new post of director of children's services and a new body, the Children's Trust. But neither the trust nor its director has direct control over the whole of the budget or the policy for which they are accountable and must deliver wholly by negotiation. There are no exact precedents for this and nobody knows how, or even if, it will work out in practice.

In Wales the Welsh Assembly government has decided against the English model and is relying for the delivery of an integrated service on the existing strategic forums. These certainly have worked elsewhere, but arguably not across the whole of mainstream services and not in local areas as small as those defined by the 22 Welsh local authorities (with an average population size less than 140,000).

In large county areas in England the marginal surplus is large enough to permit piloting and experimentation on a viable scale. In the small Welsh authorities the margins are too small. The much promoted and heralded brigading of services and developments across larger populations has not happened to any extent. There is no inherent reason why it shouldn't, but it would require the strong leadership discussed above.

No doubt some of these unknown, and probably unknowable, factors will apply to services for adults too, as the models begin to evolve in detail.

Conflicts

Any democratic government contains a range of policies and pressures in conflict with each other within its own house. It is the inevitable effect of seeking to represent the aspirations of as many elements of the electorate as possible, many of which will be mutually hostile. Three which have a particular impact on the partnership agenda are the *national/local, social care/social control* and *social liberal/economic liberal* dichotomies.

National/local

The polarisation here is between national equity and local control. In many ways this is the least difficult because, on the whole, most local partnerships are more than happy to accept a strong central government hand in policy formation. The problem is explicitly recognised on both sides. Part of the agenda of the Office of the Deputy Prime Minister for area level agreements, for example, is to reconcile the Government's desire to retain broad policy control with legitimate local aspiration. The strong central control of policy might be a problem on other agendas, notably the problem of getting public engagement in local democracy where major policy decisions are largely out of local hands. But issues of that kind are outside the scope of this book.

Social care/social control

With its social justice and social care hat on, the Government has sought to reduce poverty and exclusion among vulnerable groups, has driven forward on neighbourhood renewal and on targeted help to vulnerable communities, and has invested heavily in health and social care, at least by the standards of its recent predecessors. And it has done so with considerable success in some policy areas. It has certainly not been an exercise in empty rhetoric. The pressure for partnership and collaboration itself belongs firmly within this basket of policies.

With its law and order hat on, however, it has become progressively more authoritarian since it was first elected. As we have seen, words such as 'wino', 'thug' and 'vandal' have become part of the ministerial lexicon. This is not mere rhetoric either. The fact that we have a new quasi-criminal order – the Anti-Social Behaviour Order – on the statute book, creating a new concept in the state control of personal behaviour, makes that very clear. And we now have the largest prison population in our history, both in sheer numbers and in proportion of the total population. Early in September 2005 the prime minister announced the establishment of a new government unit to promote (actually enforce, because there will be backing legal powers) 'respect' in those deemed insufficiently respectful or raising their children in a way which challenges authority.

The problem for social care partnerships is that the target of most of this control is not the successful, affluent and powerful. It is precisely those for whom the existence of effective social care partnerships is particularly important: the vulnerable, impotent, asocial and anti-social people who have difficulty in getting their voices heard. They sometimes behave in socially unacceptable ways which are beginning, increasingly, to be criminalised. Aspects of this group of policies run in exactly the opposite direction to those promoted by, for example, the Social Exclusion Unit.

Social liberal/economic liberal

Though it wears a heavy political disguise, there is considerable tension between the freewheeling, entrepreneurial capitalism (to use the language of its advocates) based on low taxation, limited regulation and small government, and the social liberal model based on government-controlled equity, a high degree of social protection, and therefore high public expenditure and taxation. In the past Labour governments talked up the latter while quietly promoting the former, and Conservative governments did the opposite. The New Labour government in power as this book is written talks up both at the same time!

The hidden downside for the users of services is that, though the social liberal aspects of government policy have had an impact on absolute poverty, economic inequality has changed little since the Thatcher years (see, for example, Brewer *et al.* 2005). Consumer participation based on any sort of economic power is simply out of the question. There is considerable, and laudable, policy pressure to increase engagement, participation and choice in the way services are delivered. But the drive is in considerable tension with the severe economic inequality in Britain which, as we are all aware to some degree, robs many people of any real sense of power and control.

Complexity

The final factor which will impinge on the way partnerships develop is that of complexity. There is no doubt that public sector partnerships are inherently complicated. There are many consents to be negotiated and many factors to include in all of them. The cost of managing these factors and consents should never exceed the benefits they deliver, so partnership should always remain a method rather than an objective.

In practice this means a careful analysis to identify the optimum level of information and consent for each component. To take a concrete, if speculative, example: many frail people in the community require both nursing care and home care. There is an optimum balance to be found between the levels of those services and resources that need to be directed, or redirected, to support that balance. It may also be an advantage to create 'one-stop shop' access to both services. But that's probably as far as bureaucratic co-ordination needs to go. Sometimes a nurse may need to discuss a particular issue with a home carer to get an aspect of their services to match better, but there is no need to set up a systematic (and bureaucratic) information exchange or signing-off process for all cases.

On the other hand there are some service users who have complex and complicatedly interactive needs where balance and timing are critical to the joint effectiveness of the outcome. A severely disabled child living at home needs a highly interactive balance of services from health, care and education professionals, supported by services from all three disciplines. A systematically managed single care plan is critical to success: nobody should 'go it alone'.

Because the issue itself is complex, we will frequently get the balance wrong. Paradoxically, the ease with which we can now communicate and aggregate information may increase the danger of doing so. The sheer difficulty of managing large databases before modern information technology became universal and cheap was a natural brake on our empire building tendencies. If it goes wrong often enough there will be pressure to withdraw from collaboration on the assumption that it is inherently ineffective and stifling and the baby will go out with the bathwater. I have no idea if this will actually happen, but it is one to watch.

We end where we began: partnership is the most effective way to deliver services but it is not a panacea and contains its own dangers.

Appendices

Somerset Partnership NHS and Social Care Trust

An Integrated Mental Health and Social Care Service in Somerset

This report was written at the time service integration in Somerset took place. As with all dynamic processes it is constantly evolving. For example the county is now covered by four primary care trusts working jointly with the social service department to commission mental health services. Current financial arrangements for the Somerset Partnership Trust have continued as they were originally set up, although the legal framework for pooling budgets has changed. Up-to-date information can be found at the Partnership website: www.sompar.nhs.uk.

BACKGROUND

Following the closure of the large psychiatric hospitals (Tone Vale, Taunton and Mendip Hospital, Wells), community mental health services were further developed. As well as hospital-based community mental health teams, there were also special social work teams. Although these services linked with each other, they sometimes developed overlapping services which did not always complement each other, and there were different care planning systems.

The development of parallel services led to a questioning of the purpose of an arbitrary divide between the provision of health and social care. This divide led to disputes between the organisations about which was responsible for providing different elements of a person's care.

It also led to confusion for the users of services and their carers, and uncertainty about where to access services. Users could also be subject to two separate care planning processes (care management – social services; and care programme approach – health) and consequently have two care plans, two review processes and two keyworkers. This confusion also hindered other statutory and voluntary organisations in making referrals.

Questioning about the duplication of services gave rise to a belief that economies could be made (e.g. the rationalisation of buildings) that would benefit users.

THE MENTAL HEALTH REVIEW

Awareness of the above issues led the joint care planning team to commission a review of mental health services in Somerset. This took place between 1996 and 1997.

Senior staff from the health authority, social services, the Avalon, Somerset NHS Trust and Bath Mental Health Care NHS Trust were involved in leading and working on this review. There was also representation from GPs, users and carers in the review groups.

Four working groups looked at:

- needs assessment
- care programming and care management
- services for adults
- services for elderly people.

The review involved extensive consultation which endorsed the following recommendations:

1. Joint commissioning of services by health and social services to gain the best value from existing services and to promote 'seamlessness'.

2. Creation of joint health and social care teams which would integrate clinical, nursing and social work staff under single management.

3. A focus on severe mental illness, but with a strong relationship to primary care through named link workers to facilitate the treatment of less severe mental illness in primary care.

4. A unified assessment and care management/care programme process.

5. Joint use of buildings owned by social services and Avalon, East Somerset and Taunton and Somerset NHS Trusts where appropriate to promote their efficient use and concentrate resources on improving community-based services.

6. Rationalisation in each locality of NHS and social services continuing care, daycare and support services for adults, to include moving towards a seven-days-a-week service and an out-of-hours service for known users.

7. Further work to be undertaken on services for older people with a mental illness, to include the optimisation of resources across psychiatric and geriatric care, and to ensure the availability of sitting, respite and befriending services, and to promote quality residential and nursing home provision.

8. The importance of the involvement of the wider community in the implementation of local changes – particularly users and carers.

9. A quarterly bulletin to ensure very wide circulation of information about the implementation of the review. A telephone line at the health authority for receiving comments and feedback. A number of working groups were established to look at the wider implementation issues, e.g. training, day service, services for older people, etc., and a number of focus groups on specific issues, e.g. confidentiality, record keeping, approved social worker status, etc. All these groups had health and social care representation.

IMPLEMENTATION – OPERATIONAL

There is single line management of staff, but there is also provision of professional development opportunities with each person's professional group.

A single care-planning process, 'The Integrated Care Programme Approach' (ICPA) was developed and implemented across the Trust.

Extended day care is being implemented on an incremental basis throughout the county. It is the intention to have weekend and evening availability in the main areas of population. In some areas this objective is best achieved by outreach rather than building-based services.

The importance of advocacy services has been acknowledged by the implementation team. A service exists which covers one locality, and negotiations are underway for a county-wide advocacy service.

A well established user and carer monitoring and evaluation group served by officers of health and social services meets regularly.

Resource centres were planned in all localities to be centres for social day care and outreach services. Voluntary organisations and user groups were invited to make them their base and so provide a seamless service for users. The plans for a resource centre in Yeovil are well advanced.

The special needs inter-agency housing group is planning to implement recommendations from research into local housing schemes to provide a more consistent service which takes on users' views.

Services for older people with a mental illness

After extensive debate and consultation, a final draft consultation document went to all interested parties, including user and carer groups. It recommended specialist community mental health and social care teams for older people, with single management on the same basis as the adult service. In addition, the importance of strong links to the general old age services were emphasised.

The social services plans to maintain mental health expertise in social services primary care/adult teams as well as in the new organisation recognise that much mental health social work with older people takes place in the community. This enables close links to be forged with primary care. For this reason, the bulk of the budget for this client group remains with social services. Close links are maintained between the new organisation and social services colleagues.

A jointly-commissioned sitting service, managed by social services, is established in each geographical area according to local requirements and availability of organisations to deliver it. It is acknowledged that this is an essential service to enable carers to continue to care for their loved ones at home.

Respite care beds for elderly mentally ill people continue to be available in Trust units (approximately two in each locality) where this is more appropriate than residential and nursing home respite care.

Independent sector elderly persons' homes are being encouraged to offer specialist care for people with mental health problems (particularly dementia) who do not need nursing care, but whose behaviour requires enhanced staffing levels to manage it.

IMPLEMENTATION – STRATEGIC COMMISSIONING AND SERVICE INTEGRATION

In 1997 the Somerset Social Services Committee and the boards of Somerset Health Authority; Avalon, Somerset, NHS Trust; and Bath Mental Health Care Trust all endorsed the Mental Health Strategy for Somerset, making a commitment to joint commissioning of mental health services and to the development of a single integrated mental health and social care provider organisation.

From 1 April 1999 a Joint Commissioning Board for Mental Health was established in Somerset with devolved responsibility for all spend on mental health by health and social services. At the same time, Somerset Partnership NHS and Social Care Trust was established as the first integrated trust in Britain.

Structures: The Joint Commissioning Board

The Joint Commissioning Board was established to overcome the restrictions of a legal framework which did not allow pooled budgets. The health authority established a mental health sub-committee and appointed four people with devolved responsibility for mental health commissioning. The social services committee of the county council mirrored this arrangement by establishing a mental health sub-committee, which again had all spend devolved to it.

These two committees then met simultaneously in the same room, with the same agenda, and agreed to have one Chair. In the first year this was a representative of the county council, with alternation thereafter. In this way the restriction on pooled budgets was overcome.

Each of the four primary care groups has an associate representative and as each becomes a primary care trust, so members will replace the health authority members as the voting members of the Joint Commissioning Board. The Joint Commissioning Board agrees strategic direction, issues contracts to the integrated trust and performance manages the trust.

The success of the Commissioning Board so far has meant that there are no immediate plans to use the new freedoms allowed under the Health Services Act introduced from 1 April this year, although no doubt use will be made of them in time.

Structures: the integrated provider

The initial intention had been to transfer all staff with a mental health brief within the social services department into a reformed mental health trust. However, it soon became clear that it would not be possible to transfer the employment of social workers who were approved social workers under the 1983 Mental Health Act to a trust. Therefore, their contracts remained with the county council, but their management was devolved to the trust.

All other staff transferred to NHS contracts. Unions had been part of the consultation process throughout and were supportive of the establishment of an integrated trust, once it had been agreed that all staff should retain the best of their respective conditions of service. In total, approximately 104 staff transferred, including the 44 approved social workers whose management was devolved. At board level, a director of social care was appointed as an executive member.

The structure within the trust also followed the boundaries of the four primary care groups, with each locality having a locality manager and an assistant locality manager responsible for all services within their area. In each locality, the posts are held by one person from a health background and one from a social care background. The amalgamation of management posts continued within the community mental health teams, ring-fencing team leader posts to designated social worker or health team leaders. This also applied where day services were amalgamated.

The number of team leader posts increased as new services were developed, particularly within services for older people. This minimised potential discontent, as did the agreement that all staff would remain protected if they did not get a post at the same level, or indeed decided not to 'throw their hat into the ring'.

Success factors

The Somerset model may not be right everywhere in the country, but for us a number of factors have helped to sustain effective partnership working.

1. *Senior level commitment:* One of the indicative success factors is champions at the most senior levels for the agreed process. Too often the champions exist at middle management level, which may sustain organisations while things are going well, but without the support of the most senior managers it is much more difficult to sustain momentum in periods of difficulty.

2. *Clarity of aims:* Integrated trusts achieve little of themselves. However, they do put in place a structure by which services can be developed or changed more quickly and with more resources to draw on. In other words, integration is a means, not an end.

3. *Successful prior relationships:* It is virtually impossible to have a partnership without a prior relationship. How can one trust individuals only seen across the table in occasional meetings? It is incumbent upon senior managers on both sides to understand each other's organisation, and each other's pressures, and to shadow each other so that trust is built and each can rely on the other for support.

    The maturity of a relationship is not a question of how well individuals get on together, important as that may be, but how they resolve difficulties and conflict. This is particularly important in the health/local government divide, as it would be difficult to overestimate the antipathy towards each other that has pervaded the relationship for many years.

4. *Elected member involvement:* It would be difficult to underestimate the importance of political will, particularly among elected members. In Somerset the local authority members were taking a great risk in allowing staff to be handed over to the trust.

    Too often health managers see the local authority structure as cumbersome and slow, without realising that the role of the members, and, in particular, their democratic accountability, can be a strength in developing services and getting community ownership of developments within mental health.

5. *Inclusive stakeholding:* We have been able to move beyond social services/ health partnerships to stronger relationships with user groups, carer groups, and agencies such as housing, education and employment. Too often in the past they have been left out while health and social services try to sort out their relationship. A strong health and social services relationship in Somerset has allowed us to give the time to ensure a wide and inclusive partnership of relevant agencies.

Challenges

Many of the challenges were fears of what might happen rather than the day-to-day experience, but they are no less important for that.

Conflict between medical and social models: In the early days health staff could be heard to say they feared domination by the social services agenda. Equally, social services staff felt they might well be dominated by the medical agenda. The detailed evaluation and research being undertaken by the Centre for Mental Health Services Development within King's College, London, over a three-year period will reveal whether this has happened, but the anecdotal evidence so far is that neither side's fears have been realised.

Involving primary care: It has been difficult to engage with primary care at a time of great change, in the establishment of PCGs, but clearly this is one of the key partnerships, an imperative which has been given added urgency by the National Service Framework. There are now strong indications coming through from primary care in general that they feel there is a more co-ordinated service.

User involvement: A serious concern on the part of some users was that in the past, if they had experienced tension or conflict with one agency, they still had the opportunity to go to the other agency. With the coming together of the two, they felt that their ability to choose was being restricted. While most of the user groups have been supportive of the integration, this perception of a narrower choice was taken seriously by all agencies concerned and the Joint Commissioning Board has invested an extra £100,000 this year in advocacy and user services to ensure that there is representation and support for people who feel they are not getting the range of choice they want.

Charging: This remains an outstanding issue and applies only to daycare services. Social services centres charge a nominal cost for attendance, while health service day centre attendance is free. The amounts involved are very small and mostly affect services for elderly people. The income has no discernible effect on the overall finances of the trust. We have agreed to make no changes at the moment but await clearer guidance following the Older Persons National Service Framework and the outcome of the North Devon ruling.

Brief for Early Start Review with Consultants' Response

ACKNOWLEDGEMENTS

I would like to record grateful thanks to the Chief Executive's Department, Bolton Metropolitan Borough Council, and to Kelly Warriner in particular for permission to reproduce the first part of this appendix; and also to Mike Williams of Partnership at Work for permission to reproduce the second part. In both cases I have removed some passages from the text, either because the information was confidential or because it was irrelevant to an understanding of the general structure of the brief.

PART 1: BRIEF FOR EARLY START REVIEW

Introduction and background

The partners are in the process of developing their response to the Children Act and integrating children's services.

Context

The Children and Young People's Partnership has been established as an integral part of the Local Strategic Partnership. Key Partnership Boards of the Children and Young People's Partnership are developing well, including two age-related Partnership Boards:

- Early Start (prenatal to age 7/8, end of Key Stage 1).
- Positive Action and Support (age 7/8, Key Stage 2, to 19 years).

There is also a Local Safeguarding Board and discussions are taking place regarding the possibility of a Partnership Board in respect of learning which would report to both the Children and Young People's Partnership and the Lifelong Learning Partnership.

The Council is progressing the integration agenda through the Lead Executive and the Lead Director for Integrating Children's Services.

The Chief Executive is also planning to come forward with proposals around the Council's re-alignment of management responsibilities.

The partnership is aiming to concentrate upon outcomes (particularly the outcomes set in *Every Child Matters*, and the Children's National Service Framework) and more effective services for children, young people and families, rather than purely structural arrangements.

Examples of integrated services development and delivery are already in existence in a number of areas, often through secondments; team approaches; informal arrangements, rather than structure change, e.g. the development of Children's Centres; services for children with disabilities, through our pilot Children's Trust for children with disabilities; young people's services and Connexions services.

The Early Start Partnership Board commenced in October 2004 and is being chaired initially by the Assistant Director, Education and Culture. The Board comprises representatives from all sectors – public, private, voluntary and community. The Board will, in due course, consider all services and initiatives for children of the prenatal to 7/8 years age range.

Review of 'Early Start' services

The partnership is keen to align its service provision across the various departments into a more strategic unified 'Early Start' service, in order to ensure more effective services for children and their families; and to see a greater sense of children at the heart of services, teamwork and consistent collaboration across the sector and to ensure that services focus upon prevention and early intervention.

The partnership wishes to commission a review of spheres of work related to the prenatal to 7/8 years age range, end of Key Stage 1, including team structures, methods of working and also existing strategic and operational groups, and for all these to be reviewed within the context of the new Children and Young People's Partnership arrangements, with a view to streamlining the approach. We would expect firm proposals for the composition, management and operational/team structures of an 'Early Start' Unit/Division, which could operate within the context of a Children's Services Department (and in the interim, across the various departments).

The main focus of this Review will be upon the following services which are either delivered directly or support children and families within the 'Early Start' age range:

[List of services follows.]

It should be noted, however, that, within the Council, services are provided or commissioned via a range of departments, which will have to be broadly considered within this review:

[Long list of local authority and other agencies follows.]

It is envisaged that in due course a new joint planning and commissioning team may be established, which would support all children and young people's services, i.e. across the 'Early Start' and Positive Action/Support age ranges.

Requirements

- Research – present and future trends/neighbourhood renewal/regeneration – what works elsewhere
- Planning of services, including needs assessment
- Commissioning of services
- Performance management of services (monitoring, measuring, best value, review and evaluation)
- Funding and programme management

Recommendations from the consultants in respect of such a team would also be required.

This commissioned review must start as specified and complete within 8 weeks of the start date. The review will support the wider work being undertaken around the 'integration' agenda.

The partnership is inviting a number of organisations to tender for this piece of work. Organisations should submit their proposals, methodology, and details of the individuals to be involved in the review, timescales and costings together with an outline of their previous experience.

PART 2: CONSULTANTS' RESPONSE

The review will have three components, *inputs*, *process* and *outputs*, the main elements of each of which are shown in Figure A2.1.

Inputs

Our approach starts with the givens, the current stage of development, needs analysis, and consideration of an ideal service.

The *givens* are the decisions already made and the context within which the review is to be conducted. For instance, an Early Start Partnership Board

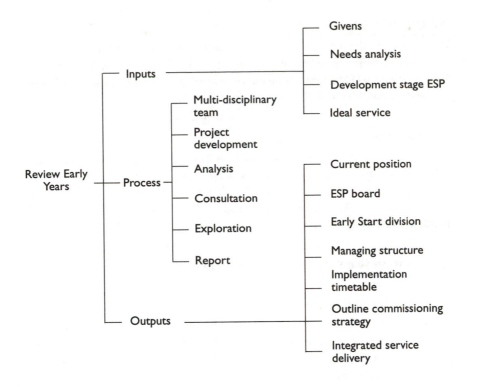

Figure A2.1

has already been set up, it has been agreed to establish an Early Start Division, and to emphasise 'more effective services...rather than purely structural arrangements'. There will also be budgetary constraints.

Analysis covers local information including demographic data, spend on the components of Early Start Services, objectives, lines of accountability, and staff job descriptions. The proposal is based on the assumption that this analysis has already taken place and is readily available. Consultants will familiarise themselves with the Preliminary Report of the Evaluation of Children's Trusts to create a common base of understanding.

[Several paragraphs of description follow.]

Process

Our multidisciplinary process begins by agreeing project development. The process we suggest would consist of analysis of the existing situation, consultation with stakeholders, exploration of alternative approaches, and the production of draft recommendations followed by further consultation.

Project initiation

The first step in the process will be to meet with the Project Board to discuss and agree the programme in detail. Following that meeting we will produce a Project Initiation Document setting out the intended outcomes, consultants' work allocation, timescales and associated risks.

Consultation

The consultation exercise will gather the perspectives of a wide range of stakeholders. It will focus separately on those people who already have experience of integrating services for children through individual interviews (face-to-face or by telephone) or group meetings, and on those who do not, whose views would mainly be sought by questionnaire.

Consultation with people with experience of integrated services

[Several paragraphs of description follow.]

We will develop interview protocols, to be agreed and then sent to individuals in advance of consultation. The questions would be tailored to the particular group of consultees. In broad terms, the topics would provide responses to these questions:

- What do you understand by integration at governance, strategic, process, and service delivery level? These are the aspects of 'infrastructure of integration' identified in the Children's Trusts Evaluation.
- How well do existing arrangements work in providing an integrated service?
- What works well and why?
- What needs improvement and how?

In the case of the children, parents and carers, and staff involved with the Children's Trust, Sure Start and the Children's Centre we will also ask what has changed, including any early impact on outcomes for children and their families, what challenges to integration have been recognised and how they are being addressed, and what remains to be done.

[Further detailed description.]

Consultation with people not yet involved with integrated services

[Further description.]

Exploration

We will distil the information, etc.

We will circulate a 'position paper' summarising our thoughts to all those who have been consulted, with an invitation to attend one of two consultation seminars of stakeholders. Those unable to attend will be encouraged to comment via Freepost or email. The outcome of the meetings and comments will enable us to refine the initial conclusions into a workable solution which we will present in the form of a *written report*, covering the following outputs.

Outputs

The outputs are the results required from the review. They concern the Early Start Partnership Board, the proposed Early Start Division, the management structure, an outline commissioning strategy, a model for the further development of integrated service delivery and an implementation plan and timetable.

- *The current position statement* – a description of the existing arrangements, a list of examples of integrated working, including case studies illustrating how integrated working is improving outcomes for children and families, and a summary of the results of the consultation process.

- *Early Start Partnership Board* – recommended priorities for the Board and its relationship with the Early Start Division once formed.

- *Early Start Division* – proposals for the constitution, size, accountability and (outline) cost of establishing the Division. This will be presented as a business case for the proposed new arrangements.

- *Management Structure* – proposals for the interim management of the services leading up to the establishment of the Division and the transition once it is established.

- *Commissioning strategy* – if our assumptions are correct, a commissioning strategy for children's services may already exist. If that is so we will mark up the implications of the developments proposed. If it is not we will frame a strategy for commissioning services for early years, at least in outline.

- *Integrated services* – we understand the general thrust of policy to effect improvements in users' experience of services through integration. We will offer a range of proposals to move forward from the existing approach towards providing a more seamless, child-orientated response which meets the needs of the child by the effective use of resources and expertise, wherever they come from, and that have an impact on one or more of the five outcomes in *Every Child Matters*. Monitoring systems will also be proposed.

- *Implementation and timetable* – a programme, a set of outcome measures and a timetable for the development of the services included in the review.

Time estimate and timetable

Time allocation

We estimate that the time would be allocated as follows, although this might change as the study progresses. We would be happy to discuss modifications to the proposal in order to ensure that objectives and budgetary requirements are met.

Activity	Days
Project initiation	3
Analysis of the current position	10
Consultation	17
Consultation contingency	3
Exploration	15
Report writing	15
Project liaison and administration	5
	Total 68

Timetable

A possible timetable is shown below to serve as a basis for the planning meeting. It assumes a 10-week period for the review, to take account of the Easter period.

Activity	Complete by
Inception meeting, protocols agreed and appointments made	week 1
Analysis	week 3
Consultation	week 6
Team meeting and tentative conclusions written up	week 7
Seminars	week 8
Final report presented	week 10

Cost, project management and administration

[Details.]

References

[Details.]

APPENDIX 3

Developing a New Project

An Information Leaflet for Project Managers in Social Services and Social Partnerships (by SSSP Consultants Ltd)

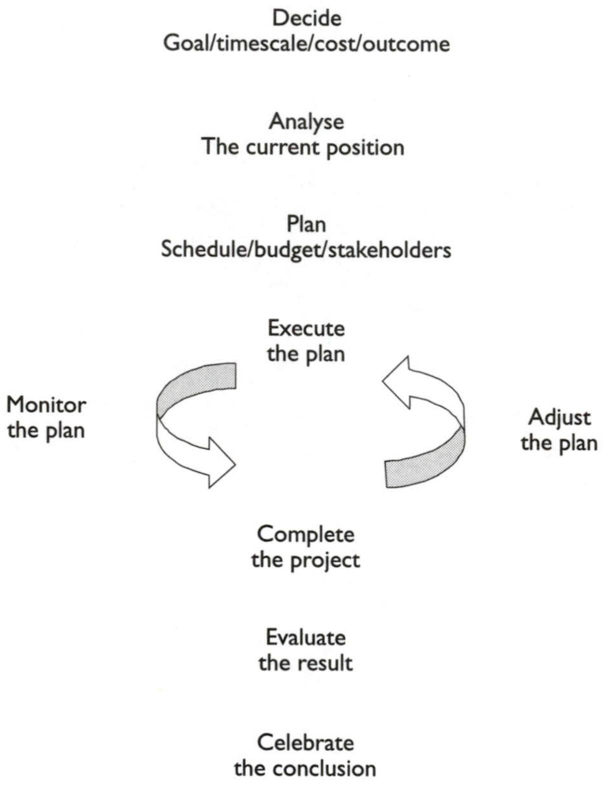
Decide
Goal/timescale/cost/outcome
Analyse
The current position
Plan
Schedule/budget/stakeholders
Execute
the plan
Monitor
the plan
Adjust
the plan
Complete
the project
Evaluate
the result
Celebrate
the conclusion

Figure A3.1

THE KEY STEPS IN PROJECT PLANNING

The six stages of project development

Decide what you want to do.
Analyse what happens now.
Work out a project plan.
Find the tools to deliver it.
Check the impact.
Celebrate the result.

Decide what you want to do

This is often the stage which is given the least attention, partly because it is the most difficult. Once the key stakeholders start to consider what they really want from a new project, differences of perception, language, even principle will emerge. From these different starting points a single set of core objectives has to be negotiated. It's no good fudging the language to 'paper over the cracks'. The core objectives have to express what everyone can live with and commit themselves to in clear simple English (or Welsh). However painful and slow, this stage has to be complete before the project can move on.

Analyse what happens now

- Who is the project for?

- How many of them? Where are they?

- What is done at the moment?

- What needs to be kept? What needs to be scrapped?

- Where is the information you need?

- How much control does the project team have over what is done now?

- How much is spent – and by whom?

- Are all the key stakeholders represented?

Work out a project plan

Table A3.1

Stages	Contributions	Parameters	Sources	Checks
Big picture	Council/NHS Agency governance National guidance	Policy context Resource context	Business Plans Best practice National and international research	Challenge/ opportunity/ strength/ threat
Vision/ mission	Users/carers Staff		PIs	Who? What?
Core objectives	Team Other stakeholders		Best value reports Benchmarks Guidance	Where? Why? How? When?
Initiatives	Team Staff	People Other resources		
Means	Policy/resource controller Initiative owner Staff Users/carers	Timescales Indicators Standards Targets		
Outcomes		Indicators Evaluation		

The table sets out the principal areas which you need to work through as the plan is developed. Some of them can be handled as a desk exercise: there is no substitute for a knowledgeable and resourceful officer(s) working systematically through the sources of information, for example. On the other hand the vision/mission/core objectives can only be thrashed out in workshops with the active participation of the key stakeholders – formal meetings may be required to ratify the outcome but they cannot be used to achieve it.

Find the tools to deliver it

Most public sector projects are complex. Once you have assembled the information and commitment you will need to put it into an operational framework which will link it all together and make the relationships and inter-dependencies explicit. We tend to use a specific, computer-based model for this purpose but there are several others. Look at the diagram below. The key to an effective project management programme is that every part of it is owned by someone who has available the time, skills and resources to do what he or she has agreed to do.

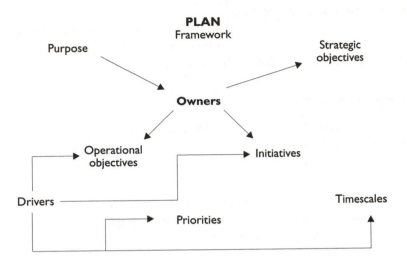

PLAN
Framework

Purpose

Strategic
objectives

Owners

Operational
objectives

Initiatives

Drivers

Timescales

Priorities

Figure A3.2

The planning framework you use should show you who is doing what; the sequence of events; how changes in one component of the plan will affect other aspects of it. And the information should be useful and accessible to everyone with a significant rôle.

Don't forget that your plan and methods need to be kept under constant review. If something isn't working – change it, though you might have a lot of negotiating with the project team and with the other stakeholders before you can sell the change. But that is a large part of what the job is about.

Check the impact

The most subject-specific parts of the planning framework are the bases on which you make judgements about its effect, but a few general principles are possible.

Make sure the answers relate to the questions

What do you want to do? Your outcome tests should tell you how far you are succeeding. If that is difficult to measure and evaluate in this case – face it. Don't measure things simply because they are easy.

Have you included targets to show that something is being measured?

Beware! Targets which measure outputs can easily distort the real impact of the service: waiting lists and vacancy rates are only *indicators;* they don't tell you much about what is happening to the service user; they sometimes even distort perceptions of cost effectiveness. There's nothing wrong with indicators until they become targets.

Don't be afraid of qualitative judgements
Numeric data is not the only kind of information! In-depth discussions with a dozen users about how the service was for them can sometimes yield a lot more of value than postal questionnaires to a thousand.

Finally – celebrate!

The team has worked hard; they deserve recognition and reward. And the project will make an impact in direct proportion to its recognition and implementation by those who need to make it work. Make sure they all know about it (and believe in it as much as you and your team do).

Bibliography

Audit Commission (1998) *A Fruitful Partnership: Effective Partnership Working.* London: Audit Commission.

Benson, J. (1975) 'The interorganisational network as a political economy.' *Administrative Science Quarterly 20,* 229–49.

Brewer, M., Goodman, A., Shaw, J. and Shephard, A. (2005) *Poverty and Inequality in Britain.* London: Institute for Fiscal Studies.

Carnwell, R. and Buchanan, J. (eds) (2005) *Effective Practice in Health and Social Care: A Partnership Approach.* Maidenhead: Open University Press.

Department for Education and Skills (2003) *Every Child Matters.* Children's Green Paper. London: HMSO.

Department of Health (2001) *National Service Framework for Older People.* London: Department of Health.

Department of Health (2003) *Preparing Older People's Strategies.* Local Authority Social Services Letter (LASSL (2003) 2). London: Department of Health.

Fisher, R. and Ury, W.L. (1982) *Getting to Yes.* London: Hutchinson.

Fletcher, K. (1998) *Negotiation for Health and Social Service Professionals.* London: Jessica Kingsley Publishers.

Harrison, R., Taylor, A., Mann, G., Murphy, M. and Thompson, N. (2003) *Partnership Made Painless.* Lyme Regis: Russell House Publishing.

Maslow, A.H. and Lowry, R.J. (eds) (1998) *Toward a Psychology of Being.* Chichester: John Wiley & Sons.

OGC (1998) *Managing Successful Projects with PRINCE2.* London: HMSO.

Pratt, J., Plamping, D. and Gordon, P. (1999) *Partnership: Fit for Purpose?* London: King's Fund.

Somerset Partnership NHS and Social Care Trust (2000) *An Integrated Mental Health and Social Care Service in Somerset.* Somerset: Somerset Partnership NHS and Social Care Trust.

South Yorkshire Forum (2000): Annual Report 2000–2006. South Yorkshire: South Yorkshire Forum.

Surowiecki, J. (2004) *The Wisdom of Crowds.* London: Little, Brown.

Thistlethwaite, P. (2004) *Integrated Working: A Guide.* Exeter: Integrated Care Network.

Subject Index

Page numbers in *italics* indicate diagrams. As 'partnership' is the subject of the book, very few entries are made under this heading. Instead, aspects of partnership can all be found as main entries: e.g. 'behaviour in partnerships'.

Author Index

Audit Commission 21

Benson, J. 64
Brewer, M. 109
Buchanan, J. 60

Carnwell, R. 60

Department for Education and Skills
        40, 45
Department of Health 18

Fisher, R. 21
Fletcher, K. 51, 64

Harrison, R. 21

Joseph Rowntree Foundation 60

Maslow, A.H. 41

OGC (Office of Government
        Commerce) 94, 98

Pratt, J. 21

Somerset Partnership NHS and Social
        Care Trust 113–9
South Yorkshire Forum 36
Surowiecki, J. 21

Thistlewaite, P. 76

Ury, W.L. 21